Tales From The O

CW01099694

Tales F

Online Dating Zoo

The Divorced Dad

Cover design by Beth Lane

Book design by Daniel Coombes

First printing December 2021

ISBN: 9798478168117

Independently published

Dedicated to my two wonderful children, you are the absolute best the world has to offer. I love you more than humanly possible, always and forever.

The Exhibits

Welcome to...

"Welcome, welcome, one and all!" croaks a discount look alike of John Hammond from that well-loved dinosaur movie that eludes me title wise. Let me have a little think. At the ripe old age of thirty, these finer details do tend to escape me. What was it called? Maybe, Cretaceous Creek or Triassic Truckstop? I cannot seem to quite recall. As a side note, this sudden cinematic amnesia is not related to the fear of copyright infringement in the slightest (insert winking face emoji here).

This man is the kind of look alike that even if you squint your eyes and do a vigorous cock thrust, or vagina thrust (we will not condone sexism in this book), whilst eating a Cornish pasty, he is still barely recognisable as the intended person. You also would look rather odd to boot because you believed that would help, you bloody fruit loop. Let's name this character Ron Gammon for now, mainly because I am hungry as fuck whilst writing this but also it sounds vaguely like the intended person of reference: John Hammond.

As a brief aside, I once had a friend who hired an Elsa lookalike for her daughter's *Frozen* themed birthday party. There were about 22 expectant children crammed into a small hall that were waiting for all their little princess dreams to come true. However, when Elsa came to the front door, it became rather evident that she had indeed 'let it go'. Elsa took to the stage in a dress that looked like it was designed for a low budget porn spoof titled 'Ho-zen'. Then the tears and tantrums started as 'Elsa' belched out *Into the Unknown* with the vocal capability of a fox with a splinter in its sphincter. No mother or child in that room were amused with this ordeal, however, the bored Dads soon stood to attention once this impromptu Disney themed stripper gram arrived.

Ron hobbles closer, wheezing like an orgy of asthmatics, in a stained white suit with matching trousers and a distinct aroma of faeces surrounding him. One hand is firmly in his trousers as either a form of protection or arousal and I am not personally brave enough to find out which.

Ron coughs and splutters out "The Divorced Dad, I do presume?"

Slightly disturbed, yet also intrigued, I reply in an incredibly posh dialect that is most certainly my normal tone "Yes, that is indeed me, old chap. What is it exactly I can do for you?"

"We need your expertise on a new tourist attraction. Please my dear lad, follow me." My one area of expertise is being an absolute basket case that on occasion is also a bit of a twat, so I am relatively perplexed as to how these traits have been translated into a commercially viable tourist attraction. However, I am nonetheless eager to find out so onwards we must go.

We are ushered into our run-down tour vehicle, a renovated Vauxhall Corsa, with a pink flame logo emblazoned on the side. I have been advised by my many, many, many (emphasis on many), very high profile (emphasis on very high profile) lawyers, that most definitely do exist (emphasis on exist), to note that this emblem has no relevance or connection to a real business for legal reasons.

The engine stutters to a start, with a lack of enthusiasm for life which can only be understood by the parents of toddlers, and we are off on our mysterious tour through a repurposed council estate. There will be no tropical island paradise for this disgruntled tourist as those bloody movies are absolute bullshit and nothing like real life. I am driven into an entrance, in the form of a woman's spread legs, like some kind of micro machine recreating the journey of the world's loneliest, solo travelling, sperm.

That was odd, I think to myself, *what kind of perverted mind thought of that and more importantly, why?* The engine stops almost in a response to my internal monologue. To the reader it may seem like I am in fact in full control of the course of this narrative, almost like there were elements of fiction scattered within this entirely true account. Where were we? The car came to a standstill and we arrived outside a large, heavily secured cage of sorts. The shit has got real here folks; heavily secured cages do not tend to house ponies or hamsters but instead hold some real nasty motherfuckers.

The lights of the Corsa beamed brightly into the enclosure lighting every corner and crevice. My jaw dropped to the floor as in front of me is an astonishing sight. "You bastard, Ron! You actually did it!" I exclaim enthusiastically. I am bearing witness to a forty something year old man furiously fucking a potted plant exclaiming how great it must be for the inanimate object to feel his glorious 'sexy time'. Whilst another, on a nearby rock, retakes a picture of his penis for what seems like the billionth time in the last minute alone.

"It is true they do travel in packs," I shout in glee as another, younger specimen, walks toward the bars making suggestive remarks designed to attract a member of the opposite gender but what comes across instead as sexualised perversions.

"That thing has got a... 4? 5-inch dick?" I ask.

"No, no... it's more a 3 at a stretch though he claims it to be a 10 incher on dating apps," Ron explains.

"The arrogance and deceit are rather remarkable! How perverted are they?" I question further.

"Well, we have clocked one twenty-something male at an estimated 12 wanks an hour," Ron exclaims with a smug look on his face.

"You have twenty-something male dating app users?" I am almost delirious with excitement at this point.

"My boy, you have no idea. We have a menagerie of the weird and not so wonderful." Ron says, clasping a slightly slimy and sticky hand on my shoulder with a wet, warm squelch.

[Note to future director: insert dramatic orchestral music here for the movie adaptation. I would also like to recommend Chris Pratt to play the part of me in the feature, trust me the physical resemblances are uncanny.]

Let's rewind a wee bit and discuss the events that lead to me being invited to this exclusive pervert nature reserve.

It all started with a divorce. My divorce to be exact. After twelve years of marriage to my wonderful (now ex) wife, my mental health, a topic for another possible book entirely, and 2020 decided to conspire together to entirely shove my perfect life up the far reaches of my saggy little ass.

So, I wallowed and cried like a self-loathing onion for a while, ate shit and watched entire seasons of *Come Dine with Me* and *Four in a Bed*. So, not a total waste of time on reflection. I now have an encyclopaedic knowledge of the winners of *Tipping Point* which will put me in good stead for my chosen *Mastermind* subject of shit daytime television. However, after a while...a whole month no less, I crawled out of the cavern of depression blinking and adjusting to the metaphorical sunshine that now poured into my field of vision for the first time in months.

"Oh knowledgeable one, how did you escape this pit of despair?" I hear you cry. Well, I started a blog (and some incredible therapy called MAP Coaching). Now I realise the words 'I started a blog' make me sound like a pretentious, self-absorbed, self-entitled cock womble (get use to that term because it may be used a lot) and to a certain extent I am. As a side note, congratulations if you got a copy of this incredible, life changing book written by the wonderful and, some would say, prophet like me.

However, I will concede that amongst the self-importance and egotistical nature of some examples of blogging there is a real sense of empowerment within writing down your own thoughts. You can metaphorically kick those nasty little fuckers in the bollocks, prod them till they cry, manipulate them like clay and, most importantly, take the utter most piss out of them.

For me, once I started to do this, it belittled those horrific fears and worries that tormented me whilst slowly eroding their seemingly unrelenting hold over me. For instance, that obsession or fear of being abducted by aliens seemed pretty weak willed at best after writing in great length and detail how *ET* could actually stand for an Extra Testicle. Seriously look at that bone chilling asshole's face and tell me you don't see Grampa's nut sack asking to phone home. In reality if you found that monstrosity in your shed you would batter it to death with the nearest shovel.

Thus, The Divorced Dad, a blog that resides on Facebook (shameless self-promotion but please like and follow), was conceived and born like an unplanned pregnancy. It was intended as a one-night stand, a simple fling, a means for me to write my feelings and weird ass thoughts down as a form of self-therapy but oh shit.... the condom split. Now nine months later, still in somewhat disbelief, I am raising and nursing (with my hairy as fuck nipples) a semi-popular comedy blog about mental health, dating, parenting and divorce that acts as a platform to have an open conversation about difficult subjects in a humorous and exaggerated means.

After a few months, my blog naturally started to tackle the subject of dating; specifically online dating apps. All of a sudden, a theme emerged within the comment sections of my posts: a multitude of women were articulating, in detail, horrific tales from dating apps that would make even Stephen King say "Oh now, that is a bit much."

I sat there in almost absolute naivety thinking, *now I know men think a lot with their wee willies but it can't possibly be that bad! These ladies must be over exaggerating to some extent. After all I was on these sites and the women had been all wonderful and I am still friends with most of them.* So, like any real scientist, after many months of intense research, I formulated a detailed and comprehensive hypothesis which was: there are a select few perverted men on dating apps, which have been exaggerated in quantity, to be seen as an overwhelming majority. Now, how to test this notion?

Step One: Become a Woman

Has there ever been a more drastic, in your face, step one? If my Lego set started like that when I was younger, I would have calmly folded the instructions back into the box and returned it to Toys'R'Us rather swiftly. My Lego Millennium Falcon, although insanely awesome, was not worth losing my little todger over.

Now, as much as I was committed to this experiment, I was not prepared to undergo a sex change. I mean the pen was sincerely on the dotted line but alas the ink ran dry, mainly due to the fuck tonne of money it costs. I am recently divorced don't forget and therefore, I am obviously dirt poor. Seriously, homeless people offer me a bacon sandwich and some change. So instead, I edited a picture of me and ran it through an incredible gender swapping app. Hey presto, within a minute I was a beautiful-ish woman-ish who male me wouldn't mind Netflix and chilling with. These were very confusing times... would it count as masturbation if we fucked?

Step Two: The Name and Age

For some reason the names that called to me seemed to be Paula, Paulina or Pauline. I mean I could have channelled my inner Bart Simpson and gone with a name akin to Maya Buttreeks, for instance. However, for believability, I stuck with Pauline, Pauline Randall to be exact. After all, I have yet to meet, in my 30 years of life, a Maya Buttreeks, although I have been told it on several occasions.

I also came to the conclusion that Pauline should be 25. This was mainly because, now at the age of 30, I am so tired and withered that the only thing I could attract is a coffin with ease. What is more, I believed that a young, innocent and naïve woman, was more likely to attract the kind of putrid fish I was trawling for.

Step Three: The Profile

Let's start with this: I am a female (teehee it is hilarious because I am not). Just to mention, I am straight. I really am, I do swear it. This would be an unusual means to find out I wasn't though. As if seeing all the flaccid penises looking like depressed elephants caged in a zoo would somehow awaken my inner, hidden sexuality.

Now for my university. I wanted to put Not-a-man-ingshire University but I felt some clever sod would have cottoned onto that. For those scratching their heads, reread it for me, I made a funny. I went to the University of the West of England. Care to elaborate? Nope. Come on? OK, it is not East, South or North of England, I presume that has narrowed it down splendidly.

Well now, what five things do I like? Let's do a rather weird combination of interests: grime music, stately homes, car boot sales and cats. That seems rather adequate. Oh, let's add in blogging because that is not entirely a lie and I believe whole heartedly in integrity. So, where were we?

Oh yes, I am now a woman...

Step four: The Bio

The bio read as follows:

Just looking for fun! I love photography, Netflix and all animals. My nickname is Jugs (don't ask me why lol). Just want someone to play footsie under the table and laugh at awful chat up lines with.

I want to make clear that I do realise this is not how women talk. However, I was sure that this would be the exact word chum needed to attract some real odd ones. Let's briefly analyse the contents of this bio for a second: 'looking for fun' to a woman could mean nights out, laughter, dates and the enjoyment of someone's company. To some men this simply means that a woman wants a dick in her cooch and no serious commitment.

The mention of photography made some men think of nudes. Likewise, the reference to Netflix had the automatic mental association with the follow up phrase... 'and chill'. However of course, in reality, Pauline meant photographing the weddings of loved ones and watching the likes of *Bridgerton* on Netflix. The nickname 'Jugs' referred to her tendency to down a jug of cocktail at her local Wetherspoons, but a fair few men assumed it to allude to the size of her breasts. The inclusion of footsie was to show a flirtatious side that was no more than a nod to a potential romantic interest, it was not, as some men saw it, an invitation for anal sex or a threesome.

Additional information? My occupation can be a dancer because indeed my hips don't lie, but the penis dangling between my legs is most definitely telling some porkies. Finally, let's select an anthem. Let's just search 'man'. Perfect! *Jessie J- Man with A Bag*. Never heard of that one but I am quite accurately a man with a (ball) bag. Profile done.

Step five: The Rules

Now to set out a few ground rules. First of all, any nice guy will not be made to look a fool of. They do exist apparently... I have been assured by sources. These individuals once deemed 'nice' will be deleted with minimal conversation made. After all, we were only looking for the bottom of the barrel: the penis picture takers, foot lovers and men who ask if you could wear a bra and send it back to them via First Class delivery. However, even these scoundrel's names will remain anonymous, out of common courtesy although their actions will not.

With the account created and now active, all I had to do was wait for the matches to roll in. As it turned out I had to wait a mere ten seconds before the first wave of matches reached me. I was inundated with cock. At the end of the first day, I had reached about a hundred matches.   Rather insultingly, female me seemed much more desirable than male me. In fact, I would argue that female me was a catch!

After using this profile for a total of three whole days it turned out, somewhat unsurprisingly, that the vast majority of men on the site were utter perverted assholes of the highest order. I was understandably upset, angry and emotional after this ordeal. The only other time I can remember feeling these emotions together, and at this intensity, was when Will Young beat Gareth Gates on *Pop Idol*. What can I say? I was invested and the man was obviously robbed of the crown. I had experienced so many harrowing conversations within the space of 72 hours that my psychiatrist needed therapy after hearing me recount them.

I held a knife in one hand and my penis in the other in preparation for exiting the male gender defiantly in absolute disgust. Then the comments started to trickle in from my report on my initial journey into the abyss. There was laughter, happiness and enjoyment being expressed in the comment section. I dropped the knife and zipped my flies back up. *Maybe*, I thought to myself, *some good can come from this*. Rather coincidently, there was a knock at the door and an envelope fell onto my door mat. It was an invitation to an exclusive resort in a rundown council estate from one R. Gammon.

The following pages are the experiences and stories I witnessed at my time in the zoo. These tales come from my time as a woman on dating apps, peppered with some stories from fans, friends and family. It is essential to note that the names of all people involved, including myself, have been changed for all parties' privacy. Think of me as a zoo tour guide, narrating and commenting on the numerous exhibits in this zoo, home to the unbelievable, unimaginable and unthinkable. However, heed this warning: these are not your regular kind of pythons in cages, nor is that a sausage sold in between those buns at the food cart. So, without further ado: "Welcome to the

Online Dating Zoo!"

Hook, Line and Stinker

Once one decides to embark on the thrill ride that is your chosen dating platform you will quickly find out that vibrators and dildos are at the tip of the sex toy iceberg, aptly shaped like a bulging, rock hard cock. The gizmos and gadgets some people shove in their every possible orifice, fold and crack is simply mind blowing. As a side note, Amanda from down the road, we can see the sex dungeon through your lower window and, though impressively extensive, it is not something we wish to see on the school run. It has become increasingly difficult to explain that those specific swings are out of bounds for children.

"But that lady is using them and she is screaming with excitement," says my four-year-old almost in tears.

"Move along child, avert your eyes and move along."

One woman, who will henceforth be known as Chloe, told me of her experience with a man and his anal hook. No, this is not a very specific blow in boxing that is directed at the anal cavity, nor is it a technical term for a newspaper purposefully leaving grammatical errors within an article in an effort to attract the attention of its most meticulous readers. It is... well like fuck do I know. Let me have a quick search online.

Oh, dear Christ! Never search that! Never ever, ever, ever search that! I repeat do not forsake yourself with that nightmare fuel. I shall endeavour to describe what I have witnessed on this 'entirely new to me' site I have found called *Pornhub*. So, from what I understand, and somewhat obviously, it is a huge mother fucking hook.

Picture for a moment you were out fishing for the bastard spawn of *Moby Dick* and the shark from *Jaws*, who was nicknamed Bruce in the film's production after Spielberg's lawyer. Then imagine the size of the hook needed for that battle against two behemoths and multiply it in size by three then you are nearly picturing the dimensions of this beast of metal brutality. Honestly, does it need to be that size? I am no marine biologist but I am under the impression that my asshole has less of a circumference than the gaping mouth of either a shark or a whale.

It is incredibly kindly lubricated and then shoved into a woman's orifice like one would stuff a Christmas turkey. From here it seems a bit vague as to what the point is as she is lead around, like a dog at Crufts, on all fours. I am going to be entirely honest; I am not watching another video to find out the meaning of all this either.

Thankfully *www.uberkinky.com* has me covered with their incredibly insightful article *'How to Use an Anal Hook'*. [1] Now what impressed me most about this article was its determination to use puns. Here are a few genuine examples: 'got a little hung up', 'guarantees to have you hooked', 'off the hook' and 'hook you up'. [2] However, my firm favourite due to its sheer awfulness is 'this is one hook that is definitely not make believe (get it?! Captain Hook...)'. [3] Come on now, these embarrassingly shit jokes are not even needed. Not once has someone watched porn and said "I am about to climax but oh I do hope someone tells a joke."

The actor stares at the camera and says "a kiss makes your day...but anal makes your hole weak."

"That's the stuff, you incredible comic genius...I am there!" they say shaking in ecstasy. Believe me, as a self-confessed comic genius, my past lovers have unfortunately repeatedly informed me that does not happen at all.

Let's start this exploration of hooks with *Uber Kinky*, immediately starting with health and safety. Now normally I would skip through this section without any fear of repercussion but oddly when my asshole is on the line (for fuck's sake now I am doing the awful puns) my attention is centred on this information as it seems pretty damn crucial. The article states that a swift yank of the hook can cause an unfathomable amount of carnage to one's poop shoot. No fucking shit could it. If I allowed the *Candyman* to go down on my anus then I would expect a certain amount of damage to occur.

Onto the dos and don'ts. First of all, a safe word is needed. A safe word? Oh, I've never had a safe word. Can it be themed? My safe words shall be 'off the hook' as it straight forwardly states the desired outcome that is as follows: for the giant, mother fucking hook, to be retracted from my stink hole. As a safe word it is also a pun which seems somewhat of a rite of passage in the anal hook community.

Another rule of note, is to not share these metal monstrosities with a love interest unless said hook has been sterilised. However, do not fret if hand washing you, or your partner's, butt juice off your hook sounds like too much effort as you can simply put it through the dishwasher. I checked the washer instruction manual and anal hooks are oddly not mentioned in the 'what can be cleaned' section. Now that is one hell of a conversation to have with your in-laws. You have just slaved away for hours cooking a lovely, hearty roast, and all the members of your family are stuffed to the brim.

Your Mother-in-law gets up and says "Bless you Sharon, that was oh so wonderful! You have worked so hard in that kitchen all day let me load the dishwasher."

Before you can yell "Nooooooo!" she has opened the dishwasher and is now holding your glistening hook of shame.

"Oh," she starts with a nervous laugh "I didn't realise these were dishwasher safe. The amount of shit on ours. Could we be a burden and do ours round here too?"

The final rule of note is do not, under any circumstance, cross the streams... I mean use the anal hook for suspension. Now the woman who told me this tale stated that the said matched man wanted to suspend her from his ceiling just high enough so that she was on her tip toes for a few hours and it felt uncomfortable. No need to wait a few hours, I feel the uncomfortable sensation will settle in at about minute four.

Holy fuck! This man has tried to go against anal hook code! The first rule of anal hook club is do not talk about anal hook club but a close second is do not hang your partner on the ceiling like some kind of sexual pinata. Who can I report him to for this blatant disregard? Is there an anal hook police force? Let me just Google that briefly.... oh, fuck a duck, do not search that either.

Also, who possibly has a spare 'few hours' they can dedicate to solely swinging from a ceiling especially if you have children. How do you explain that to one of them if they walk in?

"Don't worry kids! Mummy is just pretending to be the wrecking ball in that Miley Cyrus music video you like."

Chloe was also eager to point out to the man that he better know a good plasterer if he was planning to hang her from the ceiling as in her own, but in my opinion untrue, words said she was no *Bambi*. I have never heard of this saying, and neither has Google, but I believe it means that she fears she would be too heavy for a ceiling to handle.

So how is one supposed to use an anal hook then? The hooks are made for posture training apparently and for the slave to prove to their master or mistress that they are under their complete and utter control. The dominant acts as some kind of deviant Geppetto, yanking and pulling on the submissive's anal hook to their sexual will. Now I do not recall that being included in the 1940 Disney classic *Pinocchio* but alas it has been a while since watching it, so who knows if it was some sort of deleted scene.

One last little nugget, no pun intended, of advice from the website: go for a shit. Oddly they start this titbit of advice with the sentence 'it's time to put that scout training to good use'. [4] Dear Christ, what in the seven realms of hell occurred at that scout retreat? I do not recall an itinerary of bushcraft, den building, orienteering, tracking, shitting before having an anal hook violently shoved up your ass, foraging and fishing being on the agenda.

A final note before we end this little trip into anal hooks: can we just take a minute to gush, like a pre-anal hook enema, over how awesome and humorous the title for this tale is. The sense of pride I felt when that sweetcorn clad nugget of an idea flew into my mind is only rivalled by the birth of my two children and that is marginal at best. That is all, thank you. Let's get this the show back on the road.

Hakuna Matitties

The next exhibit we will encounter on our odyssey into the seedy underbelly of online dating is a particular pair of peculiar people. We shall henceforth nickname them Timon and Pumba, for these creatures must both be animal in origin and one is most certainly a filthy pig.

The conversation began as many do for this dear, innocent, individual who told me of her terrible tale. Her name will henceforth be known as Madeline.

'Fancy getting together for some fun?" snorted her match with a wink as he shoved his face into a nice meal of insects and grubs. I must say the woodlouse looked particularly crispy and tender on that fine day, the crickets, however, did not seem quite as delectable.

Oh boy, do I, thought Madeline naively, *but what type of fun will my sweet suitor have in store for me? Could it be a round of ten pin bowling, a meal at my favourite restaurant, a night out at the cinema to see the latest blockbuster or even a mere romantic stroll? Oh, how my heart flutters with the wings of a thousand butterflies at the many potential prospects of love.*

Oh well then, now his friend has said hi too. What a friendly bunch of chums my love does associate himself with.

And just like that his co-worker had entered our romantic little narrative.

"You look naughty," his coworker remarked with a winking face emoji.

Hm.., she ponders to herself, *well I am lactose intolerant and have just eaten a whole bar of Fruit and Nut Dairy Milk to myself. Oh, dear me, well I do suppose I may have been a bit of a cheeky sausage but how would he have known that?* Madeline asks herself as she starts to look for any potential hidden cameras in her book shelves and stuffed toys.

A minute later into the conversation: "Oh my God! Mummy!" she ecstatically yells down the phone like a pterodactyl on heat "You will never guess what?! This absolute dream boat of a man wants me to sit between him and his friend." She exclaims full of excitement "I know, I know, go pick out a fancy dress for the wedding. He already wants me to meet his friends. This is getting serious!"

He wants the heating up? Aw bless, it is cold after all. You could hang a coat off my nipples right now. He is so considerate; Madeline thinks full to the brim with infatuation and love.

Bing! The noise comes with a vibration within her pocket and she scrambles for her mobile to see what romantic prose her beloved has messaged. Well, this seems to have turned faster than an ice cream in the desert... he wants a threesome!

Heartbroken somewhat, but still determined to make this work, Madeline asks for more information. They would like her to rub both their genitals. One presumes in a manner that is not dissimilar to *Aladdin* frantically rubbing a magical lamp. However, let's be entirely honest, it won't be a mystical genie voiced by Robin Williams spurting forth from the spout.

"What is your favourite position?" they ask.

"Ummm... centre forward," she replies with hesitation, but in the bottom of her heart she knew that these once seeming gentlemen were not asking about football.

Nope, most definitely and disappointingly, not football. The two of them instead would love to take turns having intercourse with her in a variety of positions, like a sexual relay but with a penis taking the place of the baton. My Dear Watson, I do believe I have cracked the case. Call me a pessimist, but I have come to the conclusion these men are here for sex. With a mischievous grin Madeline thinks to herself, let's *have some fun!*

I am going to break the flow a little bit here and ponder a curious point. First of all, what occupation are these individuals involved in? I cannot presume it is a position which involves a lot of concentration, nor can it be particularly time consuming. For instance, two policemen could not spend an afternoon planning a sexual odyssey with a complete stranger whilst Thieving Tom (he was never destined for greatness with a name like that) loots the local bank. Nor could a pair of oceanographers find time from detailing the mysteries of the ocean to narrate how they desire to spit roast an innocent woman. I cannot believe for a second that any boss would be thrilled with this use of time either so therefore, I theorise that these men are self-employed and, in my head, run a nonsuccessful karaoke bar where the down time is massive so their surplus energy is fulfilled with online sexual escapades to conceal their intimate desires for one another.

Let's arrive back on track. Madeline declared proudly "I am more than boobs. I am a heart, I am a soul, I am a mind, I am a vagina!"

This incredibly feministic, assertive and inspiring speech goes seemingly unnoticed as they simply state "You look sexy."

Do you think that, when Hilary Clinton did the incredible and iconic *Women's rights are human rights* speech, some man within the crowd shouted "yeah, yeah of course women's rights are important and everything but you do look sexy as fuck," to a room full of silence?

The heroine of this narrative, now clearly having some fun with these fuckwits, retorts with an outright lie "I don't know if I am up for any sexual adventures after the surgery. It was a bit of a shock and it all happened overnight."

"Oh gosh!" they both exclaim with a sense of confusion and arousal "I am so sorry and here we are hounding you for sex. You must think we are utter perverts."

Why yes, yes, I do, she says internally but instead replies with "I didn't expect them to take the whole toe. I am pretty sure it is infected because it reeks like a tuna sandwich gone bad."

The sex talk seemed to cease with this latest interaction so therefore, let this be a lesson for you dear reader, if you are being harassed and plagued by unwanted admirers simply state you have lost an appendage and the remains smell of something untoward. Who knew it was that simple to turn someone off?

Outright Shite

So, for those not in the know, most dating apps have a premium plan of some description that offer a multitude of benefits for those that are desperate to find a decent human being in the repugnant sea of Neanderthals, perverts and complete bell ends. One site, for instance, offers users for the mere price of £4.99 a month, access to unlimited likes, a monthly profile boost and the ability to undo dislikes. As of March 2021, that is the same price as a KFC Smokey Mountain BBQ Twister Wrap and whilst not tasting as nice, it will thankfully not add more inches to your waistline.

However, it seems essential for me, in the spirit of fairness, to note that not all premium members opting for this bargain service seem completely satisfied with their membership as the individual towards the end of this chapter exemplifies.

Before beginning this tale, we need to discuss the fact that as well as all the sexual innuendos, grotesque desires and unfathomable lust found on these sites, there are also some individuals who seem, for lack of a better word, mad as hell at the world and those who dare occupy it.

Now I have worked in retail and, on almost a daily basis, I have had to come terms with the realisation I dislike an overwhelming proportion of the population. For example, there was a female colleague of mine called Isabelle who was unfathomably intelligent and was studying to be a doctor at a prestigious university. So, one day whilst I was making the 'beep beeps' at the other end of the store at self-service like the unintellectual oath I am, she was serving customers on a till.

It was the festive period so, as expected, the store was rammed like my elderly neighbor when her husband received his new delivery of extra-strong Viagra. Nonetheless, Isabelle attempted to make the most of a horrific nine-hour shift and even tried to make the endless stream of miserable customers crack a smile.

Then, all of a sudden, an older woman, without any sort of provocation, said in a snide voice "I bet you wish you did better at school now!" Just take a moment to absorb the audacity of that statement and then come to the logical conclusion that this woman was an absolute asshole.

Now, whilst I do concede a level of understanding of this general hatred of humanity, there has not been a moment where words of anger, nor aggression, have ever left my mouth. I feel most would naturally assume that anger would not be the initial impression one would prefer to demonstrate when finding a new life partner. Yet time and time again, both men and women have told me of experiences with potential suitors who are angry, negative, verbally aggressive or even threatening towards them. I believe it is safe to suggest that these aforementioned traits should be taken as a serious red flag that is erratically waving in a tornado of doubt when looking to start a new relationship.

The next conversation started with an innocent, but odd first statement, 'I live in Manchester, in a detached house on my own, that I own outright.' I feel we need to analyse this a bit. First of all, I understand that owning your own house is a real positive to some, especially in this day age where the chances of being able to afford to purchase your own property is as likely as having a gang bang with a leprechaun and the Loch Ness monster on top of Dracula's coffin.

The benefits of owning your own house are plentiful; from not sinking money into rent, to having the ability to convert the summer house into your own personalised kitty play kingdom without asking for the landlord's permission. This, unfortunately for a lot of the population, seems to be a farfetched dream and rightfully so is an impressive feat to be celebrated.

However, to announce this as the opening statement seems unusual and a means of asserting status over someone else in a somewhat bragging manner. I could announce that I own a Subway card with almost enough points to get a free footlong to an obvious eruption of fanfare yet more often than not I choose not to, unless I am really trying to woo a lady.

At the time this incredible opening line was received, the recipient, Clare for the purposes of this account, was on a train so she therefore, humorously retorted 'I am situated on a train right now but I do not own it outright.'

Now one can envision how smug and pleased with herself Clare was with coming up with such a witty response sure to tickle the funny bone of even the hardest, least emotional of souls. You can therefore, surely imagine

Clare's shock when upon opening the conversation, signified with a delightfully pleasant notification sound, was greeted with the words 'What an idiot. Don't waste my time.'

Well then that was incredibly unexpected, hurtful and, I would argue, way too aggressive a reaction to what had been said. Rightfully or wrongfully, Clare apologised to this man explaining that this was simply banter that she had hoped he would find endearing. The man seemed to accept this heartfelt apology explaining that he had just joined the premium plan and had only received little to no interest from the opposite sex.

I for one can understand that frustration. It is demoralising and heart breaking when you experience what seems to be an endless barrage of disinterest and rejection. I have experienced this feeling myself and it does cause great heartache. I can only imagine how it feels if you have invested money into the endeavour of finding love yet, even still, are finding a void in your love life.

Nonetheless, it felt essential to state that due to this outburst, the future of this romance seemed doubtful and dubious due to lack of sustainable banter. To me that seems valid. You cannot enter a romance without that sense of fun or humour. It is essential. As essential as a safe word in a sexual liaison with the Incredible Hulk because believe me sometimes "Hulk smash!" is not what one wants to hear when he is near a nut sack. The man was sent off with well wishes for his future romantic endeavours and she was about to leave when....

Bing! A notification appeared. Intrigued by how well he surely had taken her mature and responsible declaration of disinterest Clare decided to take a little gander at his response.

'Oh, fuck off! You time waster!' was his delightful retort. First of all, how much time did she possibly waste? She had started the conversation at 4.33pm and that response came in at 4.38pm. That is a total of five minutes, for those of you who are not mathematically gifted. I can barely fit in a shit in that amount of time. I do apologise, however, if you were busy curing cancer or figuring out world peace and you were rudely interrupted from your noble cause by Clare's lack of interest. If that is the case, then please Sir, carry on with your noble work.

Furthermore, I may have come to a sudden realisation as to why you have remained single despite being a premium member on said site. It turns out if you are a rude asshole who purchases a premium membership you just become a premium rude asshole.

The Emu & The Canary

So, you have been chatting for a while, been on a few good dates, maybe even shared a few saucy pictures and it seems to be going really, really well but then she asks "Would you like to sleep over?"

"Oh shit!" you utter "She's going to want to see Dumbo the world's most depressed mini elephant who is shrouded in thick jungle and has not trumpeted in an incredibly long time." So thus starts an endless cycle of worrying and self-doubt that builds to a crescendo that culminates at the arrival at their door.

Jessica had these exact worries and concerns as she stood in front of the door of a man she had been talking to for a few months, but little did she know the night was about to take a turn that no one could have possibly expected.

A genuinely, and I emphasise this, nice gentleman asked the young lady of our tale to accompany him as a plus one to his mother's birthday party and suggested it would make sense for Jessica to crash at his for the evening before the do. They laughed through the entire night eating food and watching movies.

What movies you ask? I didn't ask you nosey bugger. Let's make a random assumption that it was an Arnold Schwarzenegger marathon which started with the iconic Sci-fi hit *Predator*, then was lightened up with the festive comedy *Jingle All the Way* and climaxing with the hilariously bad *Batman and Robin*. It was truly a perfect evening full of fun, frolics and Schwarzenegger doing awful ice puns to George Clooney in a bat suit that included bat nips. The evening was so alive that the engrossed couple, so infatuated with one another, did not realise that Jessica's phone had died.

Now many would concede that we live in an era where our lives are orchestrated, aided and controlled by our mobile devices. Most aspects of our days are connected, at least in part, to our phones. However, what could possibly be the worst-case scenario that could arise from a depleted battery? Potentially one could miss the newest social media upload from Aunt Marge about her thirteen cats and how poor old Mr. Tomkins has not been in his litter box for a week now. Possibly you could miss harvesting your online vegetables, on your online farm, for your online citizens, of your online town, or even be outbid on that *Pokémon* belt buckle that would have been perfect with that teal shirt you were going to wear for Shaun's and Graham's wedding.

However, you probably would not presume your phone dying would spark a manhunt centred around yourself... oh wait one second, I have gotten way too ahead of myself.

You see, like any sensible individual, Jessica alerted her family and friends to her whereabouts and situation. She also had implored them to come to her aid if anything untoward happened. This is so very important to do regardless of how well you think you 'know' someone. I thought I 'knew' Taylor, my local butcher, but that was not a Wiltshire finest sausage that he put in my bum... bun. I am not often serious but please do tell someone where you are and who you are with on the first few meet-ups. You don't want to arrive to a date and find that you are tangled up within a complex plan of a supervillain, who is taking you hostage to trade for £1,000,000, without your mum and dad knowing how to find you. Not that my parents would admittedly do much against a supervillain, but they could at least report the situation to the relevant authorities who could alert his arch nemesis, let's call him Super Steve.

When Jessica turned on her phone, she expected the odd message that said:

Oh, hey you! x Did someone get railed last night? Was his dick as big as he actually said? Can't wait to hear all the juicy details. See you on Saturday for drinks? xxx Sarah xxx

Or

Hey sweetheart! Dad has a nasty haemorrhoid flare up again so he is rather cranky but you are welcome to still come round for a roast. I am making the roast potatoes just the way you like them. Mum x

She was not expecting the following:

Jess, where the fuck are you? We have been trying to ring you nonstop and we are seriously worried. Please contact us as soon as possible. Everyone is looking for you, even the police. Dad x

As soon as her mobile was switched on it was bombarded with texts from concerned friends and family pleading for her safe return. Frantically opening social media, Jess had come to the sudden, daunting realisation that she had officially been reported as a missing person. Her phone was being constantly rung by a host of random do-gooders, who left messages of goodwill, whilst her family were around her house attempting to forcibly enter. A Netflix TV crew were being assembled to be deployed to the location to start work on a ten-part documentary series and Steven Spielberg was in deep discussions about the rights for a feature film.

Now, a detail I neglected to mention was that there was a little, teeny tiny height difference between these two love birds. You could say he was, at 6ft 7 inches, an emu, whist Jess, at 5ft 2 inches, was more of a canary. Now picture this: you are a seasoned and hardened police officer who had seen the worst the mean streets have had to offer. You knock on the door of a suspected kidnapping. The door opens slowly and in front of you stands a petite, small built woman with what appears to be a behemoth lurking behind her, possibly with a slight case of morning glory.

You ask if everything is alright to which the woman insists that she is not being held captive. As an officer of the law, you are trained for the slightest indication that she is in danger. She blinks. You call in reinforcements... the SWAT team, *the A Team* and potentially the *Avengers*. Fuck it, see what *Batman* is doing too. This motherfucking kidnapper is going down.

Now thankfully the police did not escalate this situation to the next phase of the Marvel Cinematic Universe. The worst Jess had to deal with was the frustration of her friends and family who had begun to suspect the worst. Somehow, even the man who had been unknowingly made to be Britain's most wanted, saw it as a hilarious anecdote and the two dated for a few months after this incident and of Jess's free will may I add. The moral of this story is to always keep your friends and family up to date on your whereabouts, even if you are having the time of your life.

A Pants Present

Amy was in conversation with what seemed like a nice man. Not as nice as Steven, two doors down from me, who mows our lawn without me even asking him. He simply grunts "Your garden brings shame on our village and is a visual stain to my senses, you fucking prick."

"Oh Steven," I chortle "You are a funny one," as our children urinate on our flower bed.

Nonetheless, Amy had found a man who made her smile and seemed to be able to hold a conversation. A rare breed online it must be said. Almost as rare as a Dark Charizard *Pokémon* card, but ultimately just falling short, (If you do happen to have one for sale then please contact the blog page to start negotiations).

However, as it turns out, men online are essentially a reverse of *Scooby Doo* villains. Me and my son are massive fans of those meddling kids and their mystery solving canine. I will take The Mystery Gang any day over that anamorphic pork chop called Peppa that constantly evades my dinner plate. Therefore, as somewhat of a self-titled expert, I feel confident I can explain the plot of every episode of *Scooby Doo* succinctly and faithfully: a scary as fuck 'monster' does some bad shit, but in the end it turns out it was just a person in a mask fulfilling their nefarious wants.

In contrast, in the online realm of dating, it is seemingly 'normal' people who, when unmasked, are revealed to be disgusting, revolting monsters with penises as claws and bellybuttons plastered all over their faces. Their true hideous natures are masked until their real motives are revealed, which let's face it, nine times out of ten is sex.

We return to Amy's narrative. All seemed well with her man, but that was about to take a rather unfortunate turn. It all started innocently enough; a restrained and reserved enquiry that asked if she liked presents. Well of course she did. Who doesn't? Well, to be fair, *The Grinch* was not a fan at the start of his movie but at the end of the 105-minute adventure (the 2000 live action version, of course) his heart did indeed embrace the notion of Christmas and the idea of presents as a whole.

Now, some who are not so keen of this notion would state that the idea of gifts and presents is commercialism at its finest. There is no contesting that some occasions, for instance Christmas, have in modern times been far removed from its intended Christian roots. I would not, however, state it has been entirely consumed by materialism as so many cynics will try to insinuate. Instead, I believe it has been replaced by the universal themes of love, family and celebrating all forms of relationships. The notion of presents is a means to demonstrate these themes. The perfect present is one that reflects the emotions that surround a relationship and can bring immense joy when received.

This does not mean, Auntie Jodie, that I need another can of Lynx Dark Temptation deodorant. That woman either thinks I smell worse than the butt crack of Oscar the

Grouch, the *Sesame Street* character who literally lives in trash, or she in fact works for The Empire and is attempting to subconsciously lure me to the Dark side.

Now that we understand that the notion that presents can be meaningful understood, the man asked what kind of gifts Amy liked. Amy replied that she liked to be surprised. After all, if a future suitor knew her as well as he should then he would be able to find her a gift that she loved without any assistance.

Now do me a quick favour; have a think about your idea of an ideal present.

Done? Good. Here is a list of some of the obvious ones: jewellery, clothes, candles, a romantic dinner for two, a video game, the latest must have gadget, perfume and even an experience day. The possibilities are truly endless but I would fathom a guess that underwear would be rather low down on most wish lists. I understand that for you, dear reader, this could be at the top of your list but most people, for better or worse, don't seem to share your 'world view'. However, believe it or not, underwear is exactly what this individual wanted to wrap up in the fanciest of paper with the prettiest of bows and bestowal upon his fair lady.

He further enquired as to what kind of underwear and colour Amy would desire. Now, within the man's mind, I am sure his innermost desires had formulated a sexual slideshow of Amy in a range of the sexiest of lingerie known to mankind. Images of thongs, G-strings, lacy French cut and open crotch underwear were rushing within the whirlpool of his mind. Little did his naïve brain know that in reality, most women would like nothing more than to get all comfy on the sofa in some good old fashioned granny pants and watch an episode of *Come Dine With Me*.

What is more, this wannabe fashion maestro wanted to see the delectable underwear his hard-earned cash had bought for Amy on her posterior. He wanted photographs. Lots and lots of photographs. This seemed to Amy a bit much. After all, when she visited her local Aldi and purchased the ingredients for her self-confessed 'banging' stir fry, the cashier did not demand to be sent photographic imagery of her enjoyment of said meal before the completion of the transaction. With this in mind she graciously declined the gift and the conversation 'unfortunately' fizzled out.

A Big Bird On All Fours

Name an animal that has some kind of sexual connotation. Do not fret. I realise that is a rather absurd and unusual task for me to set, but nonetheless it is crucial for the narrative of this tale. I also understand that most individuals, those not on some kind of sexual deviant list, do not visit a zoo and have to seek the nearest toilet cubicle to shake one out because Leo the lion flaunted his mane the way he knows they like it. Therefore, an answer will most likely not be entirely obvious. However, I am confident that, under extreme torture, for instance after a continuous stream of children's television for an extended amount of time, an answer would emerge.

I believe the most reasonable answer would be a rabbit. Wait, don't close this book and take it to the local Oxfam just yet, I still have some more shit to say. Hear me out first. From the most famous brand of vibrator to the animated allure of Jessica Rabbit these cute, whiskered rascals have been sexualised to the extreme. I also feel cats and kittens in the same vein have been sexualised, for instance, a black cat has become the easiest and sluttiest Halloween costume and who cannot remember Michelle Pfeifer's undeniably iconic, but sexualised *Catwoman*.

The main reason I have waffled on about this, like a mad man who has downed a few litres of the best Russian Vodka, is to reinforce the fact that our feathered friends, from seagulls to eagles, feature rather low on the list of 'sexiest' animals. Hold onto that sentiment as we dive into our next anecdote.

A conversation had turned sexual within a few brief moments of a match on a dating app. I know, the sheer shock of that was rather immeasurable to me too. A woman named Beth received a notification that read 'Tell me your ultimate sexual fantasy.' Beth went red in the face at the bluntness of her suitor and awkwardness of this situation. She was also somewhat mad. Yet another man who wanted sex. However, the initial shock of this sexual forcefulness had started to fade as it had become more of a consistent theme of numerous conversations and now she wanted to have some fun.

"Well…" Beth said with a smirk "How about this for a fantasy". She mused for a while about what to write embracing the network of weirdness that had ignited within her mind. The dots whirled in anticipation of her response. She wrote 'To run free like an ostrich.' There was no means to sexualise that comment, was there?

I personally have never looked at an ostrich and thought to myself, *Cor, I would love to ruffle those tail feathers.* I was under the, possibly naïve, assumption that this was the common consensus. Yet here we are.

The dots were back and with them came his retort "I just have an image of you on all fours with a feather poking out your bum." That… that was admittedly rather unexpected. If you had asked me to list the potential responses that answer would have produced, 'butt feathers' would have featured somewhere near the bottom (no pun intended, I swear). How is that sexually pleasurable or a turn on for anyone? This man must really struggle to conceal his raging erection when Big Bird appears on *Sesame Street*.

Beth was as dumbfounded as I was. She was in absolute disbelief. However, not for the reason that may be inherently obvious to you and me. No, her issue was with this man's lack of knowledge about zoological anatomy. Now, before I disclose what her comeback was, envision an ostrich for me. Examine its features from head to toe. Take it all in.

With that in mind, when Beth wanted to voice her uttermost bewilderment, she stated "Well that is dumb because ostriches are on two feet... you moron." He was indeed a moron and her bum did indeed remain featherless.

Trump and Hump

I have IBS, or as it is more formally known as, irritable bowel syndrome. To be entirely honest with you, when I initially conceived the idea of this little book, I did not intend to announce my personal bowel complexities to the world.

Who am I kidding? This book will, at max, sell three copies. The first of which will most likely be shared between my immediate family whom, apart from my Mum, are not massive readers. I once did 'buddy reading'...a school implemented scheme whereby a sixth former would read with a younger child. The powers that be decided that it would be a fantastic idea that my 'buddy' would be my younger brother and to say we were buddies at the end of that thirty-minutes would be a gross misinterpretation.

I hated that little ass hat at the end of that session. He had as much interest in me teaching him to read as a Wookie does in having a full-blown bikini wax and that is to say... fuck all. Therefore, the likelihood is that this little page turner will remain a centrepiece of the family toilet to provide a little bit of light relief during the most strenuous and time consuming of bowel movements or at the very least be emergency toilet paper.

The second copy may be purchased by my super fan, the incredible Mr. Todd Downing. I have never had the honour of meeting this remarkable human being, however, he can often be found brightening up the comment section of my blog with his witty, and often crude remarks. I can't entirely guarantee what he will use the book for. However, by my estimates, he will most likely use it as a type of sexual inspiration resulting in multiple stuck together pages. You are an inspiration and the heart of the party, Mr. Downing. Always keep being your wonderful self. (End of shout out)

The third will possibly be purchased by my ex-wife, who will have a copy to predominantly find any grammar mistakes, and use it to reinforce the fact that she is a much better writer than me. I concede that you are. I hope you are satisfied? It only took thirteen years for me to begrudgingly admit it.

Hopefully she will also own a copy to show our children what their Daddy 'accomplished'. Though I hasten to admit this book is inarguably not suited as a bedtime story for any younger ears. So, whenever she deems the little sprogs to be of an age that is suitable to read this swear filled rant of a book (quite possibly never), then they can say with a bemused, questionable smirk "And Dad thought this could be a best seller?"

As a side note, if by strange circumstance you are currently reading this to your young child then please stop immediately as the next part, as all the other parts before it, will be a smidgen rude and may cause psychological damage.

So, back on track after that tangent to the topic of my IBS. Out of all my stories I have told on my blog the beach incident is undoubtedly the firm (or not so firm) favourite. I feel like I need to retell it here in a more showbiz manner as it does link into this tale and stresses an important point. Also, as an extra bonus, it is rather hilarious. So here we go...

It started like any other day. I woke up and went for my morning woo (wee and poo). Then all of a sudden, a belch erupted like Mount Vesuvius from the pit of my stomach. I must add this was not a normal burp like one would expect after chugging a bottle of carbonated drink. It was instead a sulphur burp. For those that do not know, these are caused when the stomach is unsettled for vast number of reasons. The most distinguishable feature is the ungodly stench which can only be compared to *Shrek*'s breath after licking out ogre Fiona...kind of swampy and a bit eggy. This particular reek was the first clue that all was not quite right with my insides that fateful day.

Mother Nature had decided to unleash the elements that Sunday Morning and it had dampened our plans to go to our regular boot sale bargain hunt for trains and dollies for the children. Now a non-parent, let's call them the lovers of life or even the lucky ones, would see rain on a weekend and be like "Fuck it, let's just cuddle up, get all snug as a bug and watch a film."

However, a parent sees rain and then looks in despair at their war-torn front room littered with the fallen bodies of *Peppa Pig* and *Bing Bunny* who are surrounded by the debris of a Lego city and the remains of breakfast. They take a deep and long breath mixed with some not-so-subtle elements of a sigh. Then they look at their 'darling' children, who are readying themselves for the Fifth World War since waking up at 6am. With another sigh, they shout whilst trying to retain the last of their sanity "Fuck it, let's get our wellies on, pull on our anoraks and load up the kayaks, because I am not dealing with being stuck in this hell pit another single fucking minute."

So off we kayaked.... I mean drove. We drove for 40 minutes to a beach. I hasten to add we live on the coast. So, why 40 minutes away I hear you say? Well, let me explain to you, dear reader. I could bullshit and state that it was because we wanted to find a new, fun filled location to explore. The real reason, however, is because, if our children decide to be total, psychotic assholes, as they so often do, none of the prying and judging public will know us as the parents of the kids that 'peed on a bush to help it grow'. As a side note son, I feel that possibly we should emit that particular talent off the CV in your future.

We reached our destination and off we embarked down the picturesque coastal path. Merrily we plodded along as a cliched, picture-perfect family, taking in the sights, smells and sounds of the wondrous seaside. It was absolute bliss. Yes, sure the children walked at a similar pace as a snail attempting to recreate the slow-motion scenes in *The Matrix*. To be honest, that was not an issue as we were not in a particular rush to reignite the epic, bloody conflict between my son's Thomas the Tank Engines and my daughter's army of Disney princesses, Rapunzel had a blood lust in her eye at the last battle that unsettled me.

We finally reached the actual beach. The sound of gulls echoed in my ears and mixing with the gentle ebb and flow of the waves. The sweet smell of fresh doughnuts and ice cream etched into my nostrils tantalising my taste buds. My children frolicked together playfully, their joy and excitement ignited the wonder within my heart. Then I farted. However, this was not a normal fart. This was a fart with a deep, deep sadness and shame attached to it. I had committed the crime of a turdnado.

Let's be honest, there is not a means to tell a loved one about a shart. I somewhat had expected that my facial expression would have sufficed as it resembled the face of an amateur magician who, in front of a birthday party of extremely excitable children, had realised that the rabbit he was about to reveal from his hat had suffocated.

I muttered a heartfelt and somber "oh no" and, like the true hero she is, the ex-wife herded the children, like reluctant cattle, into line. Code Brown had been activated. Code Brown is an unwritten rule in a familial unit that if one individual has an unfortunate 'incident' the others leave swiftly to the nearest evacuation location. However, it seems the children did not see this memo. Those two asshats were probably licking an electrical socket or forcibly shoving Lego up the cat's bum during this meeting.

Most men will claim that a swift kick to the nuts is one of the worst afflictions known to man. Most women will adamantly disagree. No matter whoever is correct in this endless dilemma I believe both can agree on a singular pain that is truly excruciating: the moment when one is in desperate need for a shit and tries to hold in the birth of the brown behemoth.

Earlier, I noted the delectable, slow trot that the children decided to undertake on our beautiful stroll around the seaside. Well, fuck me, that rather rapidly became my fucking worst enemy, the Joker to my Buttman if you will. I rushed ahead like *Sonic the Hedgehog* on crack cocaine. I was not, however, collecting rings like that blue little prick. I had my own ring to deal with and it was very angry indeed. These bursts of immense speed were somewhat made redundant when I looked back to see my sweet, innocent son, with a blank face, staring at a butterfly on a flower about a mile behind me. In that brief window of time, where my underwear was about to become a second Pompei, I hated that little bundle of joy.

I shit you not (no pun intended) with the next bit of this tale. To this moment it fills me with a delirious but hilarious sense of disbelief. If my children had a catchphrase there would be numerous contenders. One could possibly be derived from the following story:

It was early evening and as is standard I was busy slaving away under the tyrannical rule of my two-foot overlords. They had demanded 'meatballs' from a can on toast for tea. Don't judge me for that meal choice, I would much rather have had nice, fresh meatballs drowned in a tomato sauce, full of herbs and served on a bed of buttery spaghetti. Instead, I was stuck with the human equivalent of cat food.

Nonetheless. I was merrily cooking this meal of tasteless slop. Then all of a sudden, a wail like a banshee had stubbed its toe, erupted from the front room. I expected the standard: either my daughter had poked her brother in the eye for no discernible reason other than to be a knob, or my son had hurt himself attempting his 'dance moves', which to be honest look more like an epileptic fit.

Oh, fuck was I wrong. I could not ever fathom what greeted me in that front room.

My son stood bollocks naked, his chosen attire for non-social occasions. He tried that outfit at my aunt's wedding...turns out you can upstage the bride. A glance downwards showed the immediate source of the scream. Thomas, that little blue pervert banished to the island of Sodor for unknown crimes, hung like a piranha from his poor little penis. The motorised wheels had somehow decided to gnaw and thereby, attach themselves to his foreskin.

The next ten minutes were spent detaching the undeniably possessed toy in the most intense game of Operation I have ever played. I was not qualified for this procedure; one false move could have caused an impromptu circumcision. Miraculously, the ordeal was over without incident. The child, penis and all, remains intact and healthy. I really wish I could say this was the only time this happened... I really wish I could. Yet alas, this was not the last time Thomas was involved in a story that Reverend W. Awdry did not pen.

So, with this little anecdote, his catchphrase could possibly be "My Thomas train is stuck on my foreskin and is currently trying to circumcise me... again." If this one did not sit well with test audiences, then he could always try his other favourite "I have made the executive decision to smear my poop on every letter of my wooden alphabet blocks," (also a true story).

However, I am confident the winner would be the classic "Papa, I am starving and my stomach desires replenishing!" Side note: my children evidently have an incredible vocabulary.

Now, Mr. Spielberg take note for this is where the true drama of this blockbuster adaption of this book will be. This is how I envision it. Insert a slow fade here to the next scene. Exterior shot of a cloud drenched afternoon on a populated seaside resort. A toddler and Mother, with an infant in arms, sit on a bench. The Mum rustles around to find a homemade picnic that she hands out to the children. Left of centre screen a man in obvious discomfort kneels down and shakes his fist towards the sky. He emits short squelching farts that muffle his sobs.

It seems that children eat rather slow. This fact was not made obvious to me until I tried to prevent an oncoming brown tidal wave whilst the sea defence wall was dwindling with every passing second. Spoiler alert: the dam broke. I had reached the point of no return. It was now or never. I demanded my wife chuck the car keys to me and which floated through the air like a live hand grenade in an action-packed World War Two film. Passers-by gawked, one woman let out a scream and another man shielded his small son from the ordeal as I seized them mid-air.

I raced through sightseers, couples in love holding hands, dog walkers and small children playing, leaving a toxic cloud of fumes in my wake. I didn't dare to look backwards, but I can only imagine what remained behind me resembled a less pleasant, and potentially more radioactive, Chernobyl. Onwards I ran, tooting and pooping. I zoomed towards the public restrooms where I could shit to my little asshole's content.

'Toilets are closed for renovation'. Fuck! Fuuuuuuuuuuck! FUCK! FUCK! FUCK! What kind of turn of fate was this? This was the worst luck in the whole of existence. There was a fictional man who survived a horrific boat crash, overcame shark infested waters to swim ashore where he was then greeted and subsequently eaten by a cannibalistic tribe. He would take one look at me in that moment and utter "Poor, poor bastard". I mean what the fuck have I done to deserve this shit... or lack of shit even? I will write a rather harsh toned letter to all religious deities to address this unfair turn of events and ask for some sort of reimbursement.

It was at this moment of absolute desperation that I looked towards the sea longingly. Could I really run into the sea, where holidaymakers frolicked, and turn it into a brown tainted hot tub with turbo bubble power? I most definitely could, without almost a moment of hesitation. On reflection, I would have happily turned the sea into something that resembled the dregs of chocolate milk from my son's bowl of Coco Pops. However, what I could not condone was potentially wiping out the vast majority of the South Coast's aquatic life.

Instead, I unlocked the car and sat in the passenger seat unloading farts that sounded like an oncoming tropical thunderstorm and letting the seat absorb the brunt of the leakage. The car journey home was unpleasant, quiet and cold as the windows had to be wide open at all times to circulate fresh air. This was a low moment of my life.

To summarise, IBS and its various side effects are not pleasant. Understood? Fantastic, now onwards with the actual tale. There was a man who had started to a date a rather sexually adventurous, yet I am sure lovely, girl. The in-love couple had decided they wanted to introduce a third party into their raunchy bedroom shenanigans. This is where Joanna joins the narrative. Everyone will you please say "Hi," to Joanna and make her feel welcome.

The duo asked whether or not she would be interested in participating in a 'Ménage à trois', or more commonly known as, a threesome. She thanked these strangers for their kind and generous offer, however, declined due to a medical issue.

"What medical issue?" they pried.

"I am unfortunately going through a severe bout of IBS and did not wish to be trumping whilst humping," she said all matter of fact.

For some unbeknownst reason to, I am convinced must be about 99% of the population, the man remained undeterred. He stated that the uncontrollable gas and possibility of faecal matter would not be an issue. Alas, against her better judgement Joanna decided not to partake in this sexual aromatherapy and declined his wonderful offer.

Bird Watching

Katrina had a somewhat unusual hobby for someone of her age. She was twenty-five years old, tall, brunette, athletic and had a killer smile. If one was to judge her on her looks alone you would be forgiven for assuming she was into sports, partying or even potentially modelling. However, the reality was she enjoyed nothing more than a spot of bird watching on a hot summer afternoon. Yes, that is correct. She was a twitcher. This feather bound passion had stemmed from her father's love of birds and the numerous hours they had spent together at the beaches and woodlands seeking an elusive hen harrier or chough.

The truth is she had no clue about birds. Sure, she knew the difference between a budgie and a cockatiel but that did not make her an expert on the subject. This lie about her interests was made in an effort to dissuade a suitor. He had started to make sexual advances within a week of conversation and she wanted out but could not find the confidence to end it. Her innovative idea was to make herself out to be the next Bill Oddie and, therefore, form a feathery wedge between herself and her match.

Little did she know that once this obscure past time was disclosed, he would start rapping off birds like a twitcher on a particularly potent strain of cannabis. She was lost within a whirlwind of feathers in an aviary of confusion.

She had most definitely pecked more off than she could chew. She needed to steer this conversation onto a feathered fiend she at least had some knowledge of.

It is essential to acknowledge that she lived in a bustling and vibrant metropolis where the wildlife consisted of rats the size of chihuahuas and chihuahuas the size of... well chihuahuas. Safe to say the safari guidebook for her local city centre was a somewhat brief read with the chapter that covered avian creatures being rather on the slim side. With this in mind the most logical bird to direct the conversation towards was the rats of the sky, the flying bowel moments that are more commonly known as pigeons.

In a strange turn of events the man wished to escort Katrina to scout out some of these little shit birds. Now I cannot envision this to be a particularly long nor epic odyssey into the very depths and essence of adventure. I highly doubt that it could rival the tremendous ordeals of The Fellowship or the many trials of Indiana Jones. If one simply wanders into almost any town centre the feathery fuckers are everywhere flapping in the faces of un-expecting pedestrians. It would be similar to Harry Potter needing to destroy the seven horcruxes and opening his front door to a neatly wrapped package with a bow on top labelled 'To Harry Potter. These are the seven horcruxes you seek. Please break. Love Dumbledore'.

Now to be entirely honest, right now this little narrative seems to be rather innocent. A tale of a man wanting to woo a woman by trying to engage in her unusual past time. That is to be entirely truthful, and somewhat reassuringly, rather sweet. This must change immediately as it does not entirely fit with the tone of this book. I reckon we need to inject some oomph into this tale and oomph shall be injected thusly.

The first sign that something was adrift was his confession that he would be staring at Katrina the whole time. Now as a newcomer to the whole twitcher hobby I wanted to make sure this followed proper etiquette. I found the following on the website *Listen2Articles*:

The first and most basic rule is to respect the bird. Yes, they are nice to watch but consider for a second if you were the one being watched. Would you like that to happen to you? They may not be caged like in a zoo but just imagine the paparazzi watching your every move. 5

From this statement we can derive that the answer is no, this blatant gawking of Katrina was indeed not appropriate twitcher protocol. However, I will concede that the 'bird' mentioned within this abstract was most likely not in reference to a woman, but I believe the sentiment remains.

Katrina reiterated that her sole focus would be on the birds during their expedition into the urban jungle. If her priorities were a pyramid then her obsession with birds would be the peak that overshadowed all else in her life. The man retorted thereby showing his true intentions "Well I may just have to distract you with my hands."

Hell to the no motherfucker. This is where the line was drawn and the conversation was ended. It is one thing for you to be distracted from a gathering of pigeons but please do not disrupt anyone else's enjoyment of this miracle of the natural world.

Unfiltered Truth

"I am not a shallow individual," Michael muttered to himself as his date stood to meet him. He had started to talk to Sarah about a month ago, after his long-term relationship of ten years decided to storm out and slam the door in his face without so much as a "fuck you!" Sarah was a breath of fresh air. His ex was strict, cold and unemotional, whereas Sarah was almost the exact contrast: fun, adventurous, full of life, wonder and lust. The conversation flowed and the laughter was continuous and contagious. It seemed almost too good to be true and that was because it indeed was.

However, the issue came when the woman who stood before him was not 'his' Sarah. As it turns out, 'that' Sarah did not exist. Unfortunately for Michael, 'his' Sarah was nothing more than an amalgamation of filters and photographic trickery. The woman in front of him, although inarguably attractive, was a total stranger.

So, full disclosure, I look like Gollum crawling out of Chewbacca's gaping, matted and un-wiped asshole. As a brief aside, I am rather certain that was not 'The One Ring' Gollum scoured Middle Earth for. I also look remarkably like the unfortunate result of a Hogwarts student accidentally taking a hair from the bollocks of a troll for a Polyjuice potion. As well as this, I resemble a cross between the Elephant Man's hideous cousin and Quasimodo's distorted reflection in a funfair mirror. I state this fact because I am not the hunk that the literature I write alludes to and I would not like the reader to be under any kind of false pretence.

I must note, however, I am not the absolute worst in the looks department. As of yet there is not a horde of angered villagers bearing pitchforks and torches outside my bedroom window. To be fair, there is still time for my face to represent a saggy, wrinkly ball sack dunked in scalding hot tea thereby triggering mass public hysteria wherever I decide to roam. However, we are not quite there... yet. There is, for now at least, just an occasional yelp of horror in my wake.

To be honest, I may just be being overly harsh on myself. I think that is somewhat human nature. Our insecurities halt us from becoming egotistical, self-obsessed maniacs who idolise ourselves. After all, I have had a few recent relationships and I am 95% sure they have had full visual capability. However, my girlfriend's sight is somewhat debatable, as her choice of shirts that she sometimes selects for me lead me to believe the contrary.

I will now take a brief detour that will become linked further on to the main content of this section. In June of 2021 me, and my girlfriend went to watch *The Conjuring 3* at our local cinema. Now, I realise the word 'cinema' post-Covid may seem like a foreign concept to a lot of readers, so let me conduct a slight refresh of your mind. It is essentially Netflix (other streaming services are available). However, the central differences are there is an audience of a few hundred, a 60ft screen, so I can see all sixty of Dwayne 'The Rock' Johnson's glistening abs, a stereo system that vibrates your innards, day old snacks that have the texture of a leather shoe and seats that destroy your posture and give you a severe case of haemorrhoids.

We arrived on time and went towards the screen, however, I was halted and asked my age. I must reinforce the fact that at the time I was 29, 6ft 4, bearded and broad shouldered... features that inarguably do not scream teenager. To be fair to the customer assistant when someone has a face mask on it does obscure half of their face, so I do indeed understand the need to be extra cautious.

However, when the film started and the age certificate was displayed as a 15, I did have to question the cinema chain's process a little bit. After all, I last looked 15 when I was about 4 and fresh off my mother's teat. My other half found this absolutely hilarious, to which I felt obliged to mention to my lady friend that if they believed me to be 15, they most likely considered her to be my mother. Oddly, she remained rather silent after that. We can therefore conclude that, at the bare minimum, I look like a rather youthful sack of crap.

Now, back to the art of filters. The point of the former paragraphs was to highlight how I do not see myself as a looker in the slightest. Nonetheless, the face that appeared on my dating profile is indeed me, warts, wrinkles, double chins, creases and all. I have never and will never use a filter on a dating profile. However, I have matched with numerous individuals that have used a real creative licence with their dating pictures.

I do understand this to some extent. The point of going on a dating app is undeniably to attract a potential love interest. You ideally want to put your best front on to increase your chances of a successful match. That is why, for instance, I do not use pictures of me on the toilet having a vindaloo poo or sweating like an overweight walrus in a desert after the slightest of jogs. I do indeed try to represent my best self. Despite this, my current girlfriend states that my dating app gallery made me look like a drug dealer. This to be honest was not the look I had intended but it does also call into question why she matched with me in the first place.

To summarise, the allure of filters is obvious. A magical mask that with a flick of a switch can make us into an 'ideal' version of ourselves. The issue with that is, to some varying degree, it is starting a relationship on a lie. Picture this; if I said I was a multi-millionaire who had endless wealth and then, once we met, I actually confessed I worked at the delicious pizzeria known as Dominos but could give you an endless amount of their delectable onion and garlic dip for the rest of your years. To be completely honest I would probably stick around, because that dip is the nicest tasting sauce on Earth and I would happily smear it all over my body. However, to most, the trust would be broken regardless of how truthful they were about their other attributes. A lie of that magnitude cannot blossom into true romance.

You might be sat there thinking 'what a complete jerk you are, looks shouldn't matter that much. Sure, they may not look like a model, but their personality should be the real trait that matters. This is completely and utterly true. For most decent people, personality trumps all, whilst looks are regarded as an added bonus.   This was the exact quandary Michael faced; just because she looked different to how he envisioned it did not change the personality that he fell head over heels for. With this in mind, he devoted weeks to her on wonderful dates and intimate afternoons in an effort to override her deceit. Nonetheless, the lie had taken root and had become irreversible. It is with sadness on both sides that their bond never healed and their time together came to an end.

However, in a world where both men and women focus on their looks, should we really be surprised that so many people turn to technology to 'perfect' themselves when trying to attract a partner? It is inarguably more of an issue with the media, and the society built around it, that oppresses us into believing we are not attractive enough to be loved. We are suffocated with endless photoshopped images of celebrities claiming to be 'real' and therefore, making us feel lesser and undesirable because no human can ever match that level of fake beauty. It has disastrously reached a level now where individuals are unwilling to even show their real selves to someone that they potentially could spend the rest of their lives with.

Deflower Power

Throughout the entirety of history, multiple cultures and religions, the very notion of a virgin has been a desirable one. The most common reasoning behind this is the idea of purity... someone who is naïve to the touch of another man or woman. Someone who is clean and unspoilt. However, our collective beliefs about sex and love have evolved with the realisation that the act of intercourse is undeniably natural and does not have to equate to a lifelong contract.

In this new modern era of sexuality, Sabrina is entitled to have a cock on Monday, a three way on Tuesday, a break on Wednesday to catch up on Love Island, and then carry on her fuck fest throughout the rest of the week, without a shred of shame. God dammit, if Sabrina wants a dick a day, then that is her prerogative.

With the arrival of this cultural, sexual awakening for both Sabrina and the rest of the world, the desirability for a virgin has dwindled. But (and this is a bigger butt then Nicki Minaj after her hundredth ass cheek implant) there are a few individuals who still accumulate V cards like they are children collecting the next must have trading card game.

It is one of these very individuals that Sabrina encountered one quiet Wednesday afternoon after a particularly rousing episode of *Bargain Hunt* where a team only bloody well won an inspiring £100. A notification from Sabrina's phone broke the silence and her eyes were greeted with the most classic of opening lines.

Do you remember the timeless love story of Romeo and Juliet? You most likely read it in frustration in GSCE English and thought to yourself, *wait one second teach, isn't this Shakespeare guy supposed to be one of the greatest writers of all time? This motherfucker can't even spell let alone tell a decent yarn.* Alternatively, you may have watched the edgy and more accessible 1996 film *Romeo + Juliet* as your English teacher desperately tried to make Shakespeare seem 'cool' to no avail.

There is a scene within the play where Romeo gently throws small pebbles at the window to coax his fair maiden out of her boudoir. She perches on the edge of her balcony, playfully teasing her hair with an innocent grin across her face, when Romeo shouts "Oi love, anyone else had a go on you yet?" Full disclosure, this aforementioned scene did not really happen in Shakespeare's iconic masterpiece.   Nonetheless, this scene did, however, occur centuries after the great bard put quill to parchment, at the start of Sabrina's loveless story.

Ding! The notification arrived to her mobile screen and it read 'Are you a virgin?'. Sabrina was 22, so to be fair, this was not necessarily entirely implausible. However, Sabrina had led a rather sexually adventurous life acquiring numerous notches on her bedpost. Moreover, she was puzzled as to why the answer to this question mattered so early on in a conversation. Intrigued to find out the reasoning behind this line of questioning she responded, despite the unlikelihood of the situation, to the effect that she was indeed a virgin.

I was 14 when I had my first sexual encounter. I sat on the edge of a bed shaking like a rampant rabbit on a massage chair. I was so clammy that even Aquaman would not want to touch my moist hands. In front of me stood my slightly older, still fully clothed school peer. The thoughts that pulsated through my head were simple yet complex for a young, teenage male but all that materialised was the following: *Boobs! Bum! Vagina!*

The sense of expectation was overwhelming. All my horny teenage boy fantasies were about to become reality. Then she leaned towards me and unzipped my pants. *Holy fuck, this is happening,* I screamed at the top of my lungs, internally making my heart skip a beat and my beat skip a heart. My flaccid penis was out in the light of day looking like an anteater's broken nose. The anticipation was almost uncontrollable and then she gave me... a fucking foot job. My penis looked at me unamused as to say, "What the fuck is this shit?" I did not know how to answer this understandable question as I was not entirely sure myself.

A foot job is a rather odd selection to be someone's first sexual encounter. It relies rather heavily on the notion that the recipient a) likes feet and b) also enjoys the idea of them being wrapped around their penis. I, however, was to be entirely honest, not even sure yet if I liked someone else's hand engulfing my penis, let alone their tootsies. My penis stayed motionless for about five minutes in disbelief of the situation it had seemingly found itself in. To be honest, I couldn't blame it.

The aforementioned female school mate's foot grappled with my uninterested penis like a monkey trying to pick up a banana shaped cube of ice with its toes. Unsuccessfully to say the least. After ten minutes of futile encouragement and motivation, she decided this was a lost cause and I remained sexually clueless. This was not the magical first sexual odyssey my young mind, nor anyone's had conjured up, but more a fart in a gale force wind.

Now with this in mind, it is essential to note that there is an unusual subset of human who wants their first time to be special and magical. I know… what absolute weirdos. These individuals desire a so called 'relationship' and something called 'chemistry' with their first-time lover. Sabrina was much more normal that those odd balls.

As suspected, her suitor's initial response was rather vulgar and forward: 'Would you like me to deflower you?'

Oh, she thought, *I did not realise that I had time travelled back to Victorian England and met a true gentleman with this kind of sophisticated vocabulary. Dear Sir,* she replied internally, *I do indeed wish to be ravished by a total stranger who I have spent a mere fleeting moment with, who also seems to have bathed in the aroma of Werther Originals. What is more,* she continued, *I do indeed wish to be with a man whose testes look similar to when Santa overfilled his sack with presents against his Head of Elf and Safety's dire warnings. I mean, is that not every woman's dream ?*

Here is a little fun factual titbit which, if I include, means I could potentially claim this to be an educational piece of prose and not just toilet humour masquerading as sophistication. Think about the term 'to deflower'. One would naturally assume that this phrase would stem (note the plant-based pun) from the realm of horticulture.

Wrong! You absolute simpleton. In matter of fact, 'deflower' had sexual connotations decades before its association with green fingers. It originally meant to deprive, violate or ravish a woman of her virginity. Well, isn't that absolutely charming and quaint? With that in mind, on behalf of Sabrina and in fact the rest of the world, I would like to turn the offer to be deflowered down post haste. These petals are indeed staying on, thank you ever so much.

Aye, Aye, Captain

Pete thumbed through the sea of potential suitors that swam through the vast ocean of a certain fishy dating app. He had trawled this apparently abundant and bountiful mass of water for months without a catch. He watched in awe as his fellow fishermen hauled in marine beauties.

Of course, for him there was an odd nibble or tantalising bite, but these slithers of hope had amounted to nothing more than a toxic lion fish or ferocious shark. Nonetheless, it is true that these oceanic beasts hold a sense of wonder and awe. However, it is also undeniable that there is a lack of a certain trait to make them dateable. That illusive trait is the art of conversation. I concede that this is the moment where the fish metaphor has possibly met its match and collapsed somewhat. After all, I have never stared at my son's goldfish, as he swims around his little bowl blissfully unaware, and thought, *Cor, if only you were a talker, then I would have a pair of fishy fingers tonight.*

Nonetheless, Pete, like countless others, had found numerous individuals who could not hold a conversation. It was a carousel of boredom and he had started to feel rather damn sick of it. After all, he did not initiate conversation with a spirited debate about the complexities of a post-modern attitude towards racism in urban locales in the 1960's. Now, admittedly that would have been a rather niche conversation starter.

Instead, he opted to initiate a conversation with rather unique questions and topics that would make him stand out amongst the mass of men. These often took the form of hypothetical quandaries, such as, 'the item to your immediate left is your sole weapon in the zombie apocalypse... how screwed are you?' My current answer is a pillow and, whilst it could be used to suffocate the undead, I'd much rather use it as a makeshift slipper to cushion the sound of my footfall. Another example was, 'If you could pick three musicians, alive or dead, to headline a music festival, who would you choose?' These creative introductions somehow, to Pete's absolute bewilderment, received a mass of enthusiastic and engaged responses.

However, this elation was short lived as the real conversation commenced. The following is a fictionalised example of these conversations:

(I will italicise, like this, Pete's internal dialogue throughout this chat)

By Golly, what an amazing lady I have unearthed here, like a particularly rare ancient treasure. There really might be something special here. It may even be time to put Mr. Right Hand into a retirement home for the frail and crusty. Let's get to know her a little more, shall we?

"Are you a movie fan? What are some of your favourites?"

"I don't know."

Oh, well to be fair that was quite a dull question on my part, especially after that stellar opener. Totally hit a home-run with that first one. I mean, admittedly most people have a favourite film or at least a few they really enjoy. Now Peter, you must not judge though. I mean she may be a part of a cult that does not allow electronics or modern entertainment. Though how is she on a dating app at all in that case? Never mind, onwards! Let's broaden the conversation a little bit.

"So, what hobbies and interests do you have?"

"Nothing really."

Well, this is as riveting as reading a dictionary whilst eating a plain slice of bread in a padded cell with Antiques Roadshow blaring on in the background. I mean how does one not have any interests or hobbies? There are thousands, if not hundreds of thousands, of hobbies to choose from in the world. Navel-fluff collecting? Extreme ironing? Beetle fighting? Soap carving? Come on now, there must be something out there. Literally anything?

To be perfectly honest, I will happily take you busking by playing the violin with your erect nipple dressed as a tempura prawn at this very moment. At least that is something interesting, albeit somewhat unusual. Even Donald Trump, who is a complete and utter twat, at least has interests and hobbies. He loves golf, is unfortunately incredibly active on social media and is, without fail, always up for a not so healthy bout of racism like any other knuckle dragging prick. Fuck my actual life! Is there anyone who knows how to have an actual conversation around here?

And so on and so on went these fruitless conversations until Pete decided to partake in a more interesting past time, like needlessly bashing his head against a wall until he blacked out or trying to initiate a conversation with an incredibly slow drying can of paint.

Pete had not been made aware that gathering information about a potential partner was not dissimilar to uncovering the launch codes for a nuclear missile silo in Soviet Russia. It was tedious, treacherous and sometimes as fun as a hard electric shock to the asshole. How can a relationship be formed when the conversation had as much energy as elderly Auntie Maude after a gang bang with her local rugby team? The answer is it cannot.

Eventually Pete would move on and eventually find a woman called Megan who would erupt his neurological pathways with enigmatic electrical impulses that pulsated throughout his entire body. They later married and continue, to this day, to have conversations that make them both beam with enthusiasm and cackle uncontrollably with laughter. As for the former women Pete spoke to, he was unsure about their present circumstances. However, he did wish them the best in their future endeavours to find a first mate on the treacherous online seas and *now*, he thought, *at least they can use sailing as an interest in a conversation starter.*

An American Sniffer in

Sainsburys

Full disclosure: I have not one clue about the nationality

of the titular sniffer of this tale. However, as evidenced in

the prehistoric influenced introduction, I am not overly

shy of parodying pop culture that is incredibly important

to me. Therefore, the inclusion of a somewhat nonsensical

reference to one of my personal favourite horror movies

about a fur covered wolf man, seems rather in line with

the standards I have set beforehand. What I am certain of,

however, is that this sniffer was indeed loose in the aforementioned popular supermarket chain and no one had a silver bullet on hand to put him down.

The supermarket: whilst unquestionably a place of dread and fear for most of the general public, only seconded by the legalised torture chamber that is the dentist, is also undeniably a modern miracle. Now, instead of travelling to countless grocery stores and market stalls, we can find everything our hearts could ever desire, from wine to chocolate (that particular window of selection may show where my life priorities lie), within the cold, concrete walls of our local supermarket.

However, out of all the stock of these behemoth storefronts, there is one item that stirs, thrills and chills inside even the most disheartened consumer. I will hold the metaphorical microphone out towards you, the reader, so you can bellow your answers to me.

"Hello little Samantha! Your Mummy tells me you have an answer for me. If you could just stop rubbing your snot into your sleeve for one second, that would be absolutely fabulous. Your answer is... toys. Oh, I am so, so, very sorry sweetheart but that is incorrect."

"Good afternoon, Lauren. You are drunkenly shouting alcohol at me with a wine glass in hand. That is not even in the ball park unfortunately. Have a sit down for me until the room decides to stop spinning."

"Gerald! You have the wisdom of many, many years upon your shoulders. Please old fella, enlighten me with your intelligence. Clothes... oh Gerald, so close, but we need to be a bit more specific. Go have a lovely cuppa and a nice cake, I have got this covered."

I am now withdrawing my metaphorical microphone and will reveal the real answer. After all the mic is a rental and I cannot afford the fine if it is damaged, at least not until this book is a hit. I will warn the reader now that the answer is obvious. You will be most displeased and kick yourself up the proverbial buttocks when it is revealed. The answer is (please imitate a drum roll here via a means of your choosing for dramatic effect) ... socks.

Well, I presume that to be the general consensus, as the asshat that plagued our next heroine, Emma, can most likely be found violently masturbating into the fabric foot coverings in aisle seven on most weekdays. His sock obsession was first revealed to Emma when she was asked to wear Sainsbury's socks for a week before a face-to-face encounter could occur. Now, I am sure you're asking yourself, like I was, why the fuck is that an essential requirement? I have never thought *to myself Wow, this woman is perfect for me but, wait one second, those socks have only been worn for two months and four days. Next!* I mean, to be entirely honest, socks tend to play a very limited role in my selection of a partner, but I may just be an unusual human being.

Well, as it turns out, he wanted them to be sent to him... so he could intake the scent and swirl it around in his nostrils like a fine wine. Take that in for a while for me, as there are more bombshells to follow.

With this scent, he would assess if she was a suitable date for him. Move aside Wolverine, there is a new leader of the *X-Men* and his name is The Scent. With one whiff of a sock, he can determine that a potential suitor has two sugars in her tea, is a massive fan of *The Fresh Prince Bel Air*, takes thirty minutes to walk to work and her favourite Chinese dish is sweet and sour lamb with a side of noodles. It is a real skill and talent to be honest. I, for one, could only determine whether someone needed to wash their feet from a whiff of a sock, not their entire medical history.

Emma, who was surely fearful of what dark secrets his nose could detect, cunningly sent him some unworn socks. Unfortunately for him, his sniff centred superpower must have been hit by some kind of scent-based kryptonite on that faithful day and he was tricked into accepting a date. At said date, he arrived with no wallet.

This would deter some men who would declare it to be a ruined date that should be seen as an unfortunate loss.

Instead, The Scent wanted to make the most of this disastrous start to a date. He declared he'd rather leave the drinks behind and lick Emma's feet instead. As a romantic gesture, this is inarguably second to none that only a fool would decline. However, Emma declined with haste. She is no fool and therefore one must presume her sock selection for that fateful eve was under the required three-month stench collection requirement.

A Rocky First Date

When Lorelai's tale was first submitted to me, it started with the line 'I promise you, this actually happened to me.' When I first saw that line, I knew what I was about to read would be rather extreme. You see, I have read countless submissions that, to the uneducated in the matter, would seem farfetched and unbelievable in content. However, no one felt the need to swear to me their account was the truth.

Now, with that knowledge in mind, one would expect the highly unusual or remarkable. For instance, that the tale that followed was about Lorelai's time at a unicorn ranch where she fell in love with the handsome ranch hand that under the light of the full moon morphed into a ferocious werewolf. Alternatively, it could be the case that her man had taken her back to his old, ancestral home to meet his family who, as it turns out, were no longer of this world.

The reality of Lorelai's story somehow exceeds and surpasses even those hefty expectations. Neither J.K. Rowling, Stephen King, J.R. Tolkien, or any other literary giant, could ever have written the horrific and unfathomable nature of what happened on this most dreadful of dates.

Lorelai, by her own admission, is not a cliché-ridden girly girl. She despised fake eyelashes, plump eyebrows and the rest of that, in her words, beauty 'crap'. She had worked as the sole female in an otherwise all male environment, the one woman in the sausage factory if you will. She had become acquainted with, and sometimes even had to endure, the endless tirade of banter that was often at her own expense. It is important to bear this piece of information in mind, as it highlights how far the following events must have pushed a woman, who was accustomed to male banter, towards the brink.

A little bit more background information for you to digest with a nice cup of tea or whatever beverage your heart desires. To start with, Loralai was 5ft 7 (which made her about 5ft 10 in heels) and has, a self-confessed, enormous chest. In fact, the men she worked with would not be able to recount a singular facial detail about her as it is safe to say that they had other visual priorities.

Lorelai's female friends had tormented and bullied her for a solid twelve months to brave a blind date. She eventually, yet reluctantly, conceded. She was dolled up, under the strictest of supervision of her friends, and sent towards her doom... I mean the man of her dreams... at her local restaurant.

At the bar she stood for what felt like an eternity waiting for her knight in shining armour to ride in on a white horse. Admittedly the restaurant most likely had a 'no horse' policy and so he would have to park his horse in a nearby stable or field. To pass the time, she chatted to the friendly barmaid until her world was about to falter and alter for the worst.

For in walks through the door the Seven Dwarf's smaller and less refined cousin: Chavvy. He is donned in what most would not consider suitable attire for a date; football shirt and work trousers. Not to be shallow, Lorelai decided that his choice of clothes and the lack of tallness would not be cause to terminate the date. No, reasons for the termination of this rendezvous would come all too soon.

He struts over like a man who was worth a billion bucks and strikes Lorelai's behind with a firm hand. A confident start, that is for sure. He snorts like the half human, half swine he is, "I am Paul and all your dreams have come true today darling. I can see you are looking for something to sit on, how about my face?"

Each individual cell from Lorelai's head to toe screamed "run!" Yet, ever the optimist, she persevered and stuck with this ever-evolving awful situation. She sat down with drink in hand and so commenced a 45-minute TED talk about Paul presented by Paul to an audience of Paul. During the interval, whilst Paul rehearsed his lines for the latter half of the talk, Lorelai announced she was headed to the bar.

The inquisitive barmaid from earlier asked "What would you like, you lucky lady?"

Lorelai retorted with a smirk "I will have a white wine please and he will have a bottle of pop and a bag of crisps for the journey home."

The barmaid chuckled at her misfortune and went to pour the drinks. Lorelai turned and there, like a horror movie villain there, as silent as an empty library, stood Paul. Unlike his fellow horror movie brethren, Paul had no intention to stab her to death, unless we count the desire to thrust his flesh sword into her. Instead, Paul took his vacant, brainless head and shoved it between her ample breasts. He proceeded to motorboat them in full view of the restaurant and, to conclude, blew the loudest, most grotesque raspberry humanly imaginable.

The world descended into slow motion as confusion blurred Lorelai's perception of reality. How the actual fuck does a human believe that to be suitable behaviour? As the confusion settled and the realisation of what had occurred kicked in, Lorelai's main emotion became clear: she was fucked off. This human... no, this animal... no, this anamorphic turd, had assaulted and embarrassed her. Lorelai was not a violent woman; she would never hit another human. However, as discussed, he was not human, but an absolute turd. Lorelai channelled her inner Bruce Lee and struck the oaf in the chin with the force of a thousand bricks.

Down the turd fell onto the filth of the floor and the restaurant erupted into a standing ovation. Embarrassed and hurt, the little mutt who was all bark and no bite, stood and wanted to start a confrontation. As Lorelai was about to take off her heels to start round two, a crowd had assembled and ushered the defeated cock womble out of the restaurant.

Lorelai was left to calm down and remained at the bar till closing time where she recounted, the now hilarious, antics of her blind date with the staff and fellow diners. When the restaurant closed, she was booked a taxi. The taxi driver came to the door of the restaurant and shouted "Taxi for Balboa!"

As for Paul, well he sent Lorelai a 'heartfelt' text in the morning. In the text he mentioned that he had bit through his tongue at the restaurant during their impromptu boxing match. However, Lorelai was in luck as he would allow her a second chance... after all he had another swell that he would like to share. That swell was indeed never shared other than, one would think, with Paul's hand.

Tall Tales

Erin was tall. That was a fact. An undeniable and unavoidable fact that she had come to terms with since she was about 12. At 13 she had cast shadows over her fellow class mates, both male and female. She was teased and bullied with such 'classic', 'creative' and 'hilarious' remarks as "How is the weather up there?" or simply being called 'giraffe girl'.

Fast forward to the present day and those hurtful remarks have blossomed into compliments. Her tall stature had now become a desirable and sought-after asset by her numerous, salivating potential suitors. At 6ft 2 inches, well-built and athletic, she practically had men wanking into her Mum's garden's flower pots to be with her.

Now, to some this may sound perfect in some regards. However, her alluring height came with a curse. (A note for the makers of this audio book; insert a clap of thunder and ominous music over Stephen Fry's narration here). It was like a wicked witch under a half crescent blood moon on the eve of her birth had uttered this curse:

"Daughter of Brenda and Paul! Ye shall be blessed with unbelievable height, but cursed to walk this Earth banging thy head on low ceilings and unable to date anyone below

6ft without intercourse looking like a monkey scrambling up a rather large banana tree."

(Excuse me, audio book creators could you please insert a witch cackle here. I am really making those sound effect technicians work for their wage with this tale.)

With those words given breath, the curse was set in stone. Little did the witch know that, rather conveniently, most dating platforms would ask their users to display their height on their profiles. The witch was flummoxed and subsequently defeated. *Ding Dong! The witch is dead!* the villagers happily sung merrily out of the windows of Erin's village. The curse was broken and a 'happily ever after' was in sight.

This seems like a natural conclusion to our tale and I could be forgiven for prematurely ending this chapter here. I could use this time to order a KFC bargain bucket and devour the contents in a nice hot bath. However, there is a slightly unfortunate twist to this narrative.

For a brief second have a think as to what criteria would need to be met for a lie to be successful. Now, take that list and mentally shred it into figurative confetti, because the likelihood the topic I want to talk about featured on it is non-existent. This is not because it is unthinkable, or unusual. In fact, it is the exact opposite. Instead, it is too obvious. So much so, that the notion that someone would neglect this facet of a successful lie is ridiculous.

The issue with Erin's match's lie was that, from the moment she laid eyes on him, it automatically unravelled and revealed itself as a falsehood. The 6ft 4in, muscular ex-marine would, in reality, not even graze her nipples if he was in heels. This prompts the question: why bother with this charade about your height if your desired outcome is to meet the individual, thereby revealing your lie?

This is a rather difficult lie to maintain as the math is rather simple and effective when face to face: if Erin is 6ft 2in, and an individual is shorter than Erin, then said individual is not 6ft 4in. That is unless this elaborate scheme involved the consistent use of stilts to mask the evident height deficit. However, this does seem rather impractical and also would mean one would have to forfeit some of life's exclusively bare footed pleasures such as swimming or trampolining.

It is also rather essential to note that the commencement of this union would now be based on a lie. How can a relationship be built on the flimsy foundational bricks of a lie? Well, as it turned out for Erin, it couldn't. She had one drink, rested her empty pint glass on her date's perfectly positioned head and slipped away into the middle of the night.

DR. Date

Gwen was 18 and had started her first term at her dream choice of university. She had started to tick off the student bucket list; she had drunk a lot, made new best friends and even, on the odd occasion, studied. She had not had, however, that most relished of student experiences: the, often disastrous, one-night stand. She was unsure about her desire to have this fulfilled. After all, she had always believed that sex should be meaningful and have worth. Her friends teased her often about this matter and therefore, she became determined to tick this off her bucket list with immediate effect. Thus, the world of online dating beckoned.

Gwen was intelligent, pretty and rather hilarious too, so the offers to Netflix and chill were abundant. Unfortunately for Gwen, there had developed a slight malfunction in her 'let's have casual sex with a stranger to appease my friends' plan. The issue was that her front bottom had decided to rather effectively go on strike. However, instead of homemade placards blazoned with the words 'penis no, we ain't a ho', to reflect her inner turmoil about the ordeal, her vagina decided to be much more practical: it developed a horrendous infection. Her local doctor was baffled. She could not fathom how it had occurred, nor what would be the best means of treatment. She settled on prescribing Gwen a course of antibiotics in the hope that this would cure her troubles.

So, with somewhat obviousness, it is fair to state that sex was a firm no for the moment. However, this did not halt Gwen's search for a man. As it turned out she was fond of the attention from the numerous men and had struck decent conversations with a few. She wanted this to continue so she decided to carry on using multiple dating apps. Inevitably, a few presumptuous souls asked about the potential of intercourse to which Gwen simply countered with a swift message that read 'lady problems'. No more details were needed and no more questions were asked after that was mentioned.

Well, that was the normal reaction, but then there was Steve's reaction. "What is up with your pussy, baby?" Steve asked with the bravado and charisma one can find in the chav subset of humanity. Irritated with his use of the word's 'baby' and 'pussy', Gwen thought she would tell him the whole truth.

"My pussy has a disgusting infection, baby," she ironically retorted.

"Aw sweet cheeks that is too bad. Does it hurt?" he stated, with what seemed like a sense of genuine compassion, mixed and shrouded within the chav like exterior of his words. Gwen was struck with a deep feeling of regret for judging him too soon and replied honestly:

"It hurts a fair bit and to be honest does not look nice," she replied sincerely.

As it turned out, Steve was not dissimilar to a mischievous fox. He wanted to be inside that sack of rubbish no matter how much it stunk. "Sweetheart, show me!" he said with a curious amount of enthusiasm.

"Oh wow, Dr Christian Jessen from the TV show, *Embarrassing Bodies*. I did not realise that online dating apps had become the new platform for the show?"

For those not in the know, *Embarrassing Bodies* is an illogical Channel 4 show where members of the general public, who are too afraid or embarrassed with their 'embarrassing' health issues to see a healthcare provider, turn to. These individuals opt to broadcast their humiliating, mortifying, and sometimes even degrading issue to the entire nation and which, let's be honest, seems rather irrational. Let's imagine I had a ball sack that fell to the floor and thus caused me to fall over on a regular basis. I, for one, would not wish to televise it to the likes of my elderly work colleague, Barbara, whilst she sits with her dinner and watches Channel 4.

I mean, I have shown my local doctor but, as you are evidently also a medical professional, I would love a second opinion. Please feel free to have a gander around the mulberry bush, Gwen thought in this humorous, fictional conversation I am writing.

"So, what are your thoughts, doc?" which, in my imagination, is said as an impersonation of Bugs Bunny.

Steve uttered with the utmost amount of sadness "It must be awful not to have sex."

"Well, to be honest, it was not at the forefront of my mind, Steve. I was more concerned about the fact it burns, itches and is reminiscent of a pustular volcano. With that in mind, Doctor Steve what would your recommended course of treatment be?"

"Have you tried having anal or oral?" he enquired.

"Well, no I have not. Oddly that never crossed my mind. I was foolishly taking these antibiotic tablets, like an absolute mug. I mean, my vagina currently looks like a doner kebab that has been left in the sun so, to be entirely honest, I don't believe a cock in the bum or mouth is the solution but... then again you are the expert... let me get the lube."

Of course, Gwen did not meet Steve nor take his recommended medication. I am thrilled to announce that she has made a full recovery. She did indeed have sex at university but it was with her boyfriend who she would marry a few years later. As for Steve, he is still an infection on this Earth and no amount of cock in his bum or mouth will fix that.

Soccer Sexist

Three facts to know about me: the first is that I am weird and the second is that I am not an American citizen. Let me elaborate so not to isolate an entire country. It is not that I dislike America at all... in fact I adore Walmart, Orlando and numerous more of the country's abundant offerings. Rather, I reinforce my nationality simply because I need to excuse my use of the term soccer instead of football.

You see, the yet undisclosed third fact will explain this intended dialectical mishap: I love alliteration. Now, to be perfectly honest, this should have been evident from a one crucial factor: my secret identity i.e. 'The Divorced Dad'. I am about to hit the audience with a nuclear bomb of truth: I am not Divorced. I am still happily married. This is all a farce and charade. I cannot live this lie any more.

Put down the pitchforks and torches, ladies and gentlemen. Oh, and Gerald, put down the... is that a flip flop? Seriously? What kind of damage did you expect to inflict upon me with that? Oh, the buckle is metal. Well then, that does indeed change the situation. Let's put the weapon of immeasurable destruction down and talk.

Obviously, I jest to some extent. Me and my ex-wife are indeed separated, however, due to finances, time and lack of necessity, our divorce has not been finalised. Therefore, the reasoning behind the self-acclaimed title,

The Divorced Dad, is simply due to alliteration and it rolls off the tongue as well as a Rolo.

I wish this obsession with alliteration was the weirdest habit I had surrounding the written word. Take another look at the alias The Divorced Dad for me. Those who are astute may notice that there is a distinct lack of descenders in that title. "What the fuck is a descender?" I hear you cry in confusion and dismay. For the longest of times, I use to call them 'danglies', these are the portion of a lower-case letter that falls behind the base line of a font. I am terrified of them. In layman's terms these are the letters: p, q, y and g. I can sometimes handle j on a good day, though only if my big boy pants are feeling extra secure.

Now, I am a strong believer that no one should be ridiculed for any particular phobia, no matter how absurd these seem to be to outsiders. Most phobias are incredibly personal and can stem from immense trauma that can be both overwhelming and debilitating. However, to be frank, this one is fucking ridiculous.

This weirdness started when I went to university in 2010. As a preface to this, let me write a brief bit of background information. I have dyspraxia, a condition where one is in a constant wrestle with their lack of coordination. I was also not a smart child. This is exemplified rather effectively by the following anecdote: I once attended the school recorder club because I legitimately believed that it would involve me recording fellow pupils' conversations like some kind of porky, uncool super-spy. Yeah, I was dumb. Therefore, it took a lot of hard work and dedication to achieve a set of commendable results that landed me a place in a respected university.

It seemed that my entire academic journey culminated in what I achieved at university. This was an insane amount of pressure to achieve. As well as this, I soon realised that the university lifestyle was not the slice of heaven I had dreamt of. In fact, I would state that I found it hell on Earth. It was stressful, overpriced and un-engaging, to a throw a few adjectives around that applied to my experience. Yes indeed, this was a bit of a kick in the bollocks after the fantastic time I had at Sixth Form.

Now, let's fast forward to the final semester of this educational rodeo. This is where we are interrupted by a frantic, loud and heavy knocking at the door. "Who is it?" I beckon. Well, if its not the drunken lout OCD and his equally unpleasant friends, depression and anxiety, shit faced and ready to ruin your quiet evening in.

"Well, you might as well come on in guys but please try not to fuck my house up... what's that? Anxiety has puked on the carpet and depression has broken the TV. Well, isn't that fucking brilliant."

This combination of these asshole conditions made me believe that these descender letters made my work look unprofessional and visually unappealing. This made the essential task of essay writing rather difficult.   The synonyms on Microsoft Word became my best friend and ally against the war on the danglies.

I could not, for instance, use the term 'shitty cry baby' but I could (searches synonyms) use 'detestable individual who shed tears like an infant'. This made me make sentences unnecessarily complicated, however, the real issue came with names and quotes. How the hell are you supposed to write the name Gregory Pyque when the very sight of the inconsiderately named knobhead in your work makes you feel sick to the stomach? The answer is you don't use it. Instead, you scour the internet for another quote from someone whose mother had the foresight, and decency, to be a bit more considerate with her naming conventions.

Moreover, how do you quote something when it contains those fear inducing letters? You write them like this:

'Vibert believed that' the world 'was consumed with these biases about the third world and this was' reflected 'in the cinema of the time'.

So, in that sentence, I interrupted the citation to substitute the author's dangly word 'society' for my own 'the world'. I would then continue until the next descended letter caused me to repeat this process.

Now, at the time to me, this was a mere weird and unusual peculiarity. On reflection, I was stressed, scared and consumed in an obsession to obtain a 2:1 and the fear of what would happen if I did not. In the end, I did achieve a 2:1 which acted as a massive fuck you to the OCD that has had a hold over me for most of my life. However, even now, typing a dangly letter in a formal piece of prose makes me feel uncontrollably uncomfortable. Nonetheless, as evidenced in this book I have overcome this 'fear' and can write the unthinkable letters if needed.

Off the side track and back to the narrative. There once was a rather sexist individual. Laura had met him online and he had asked her about her hobbies. She stated that she was an avid football fanatic who was also a rather talented striker to boot. This statement was met with a sneer followed with the short sentence "I doubt it." Irritated, Laura elaborated that she would have him know that she was a better footballer than even some men.

This is a fair statement that could be, objectively, true. At the very least, it was not for a man, who knew nothing of her sporting ability, to judge based on his preconceived biases towards female sport. After all, female football has now become one of the most rapidly growing sports in the world even starting, albeit slowly but surely, to rival the male equivalent.

Nonetheless, this imbecile, who most likely took a brief moment from digging a finger inside his bum hole, sent a rather 'hilarious' GIF to Laura. This GIF was of a chimpanzee in the national England football kit pointing and laughing. This was followed with a somewhat rather insulting and odd question: "How many keepie uppies can you do? ... in one go, not adding all your attempts together?"

I like football, but I must concede I do not consider myself to be an expert on the subject to any extent. However, I do believe that keepie uppies are not necessarily a reflection on the quality of one's ability on the pitch. Much the same as how one cannot judge someone's sexual prowess by their ability to open a condom packet in the dark. It is not the main event, but a mere side show.

Laura answered the wannabe Beckham's question honestly but this was met with instant dismissal, as it was deemed a mere fabrication. With this, Laura decided to block this idiot. I endorse this action because I feel his actions indicate that he is a mere sperm splodge on a dirty rug. Yes, the use of danglies was entirely worthwhile to describe this dickhead.

Picnic Dick

We have had the subjective pleasure of examining a fair few of these terrible tales to start to make some educated assessments about the online dating world. It would seem a common theme within these narratives thus far is as follows: a woman will reach a limit, oh say roughly around the 79th dick pic or crude comment, where one decides to end these niceties and instead fuck around with these assholes.

As evidence to support this highly scientific hypothesis, I present the following account of Tobias and Charlotte. It all started with the unusual question "What flavour is your vagina?" Charlotte had the undeniably natural 'what the actual fuck' reaction one would have in that situation. The alternative, of course, is to present one's vagina like a party selection of dips for the said man to dunk his balls into.

I am sure, like myself and Charlotte, one has never really had to ponder this question before. Admittedly for me, this is because I strangely, as a male, lack a vagina, though I have been assured by a few of my female friends this is not a common question thrown towards them. One friend can be quoted in saying "fuck off did someone ask that. What an absolute weirdo."

A weirdo indeed. Most women are not forced to think about their female organs as if they were the newest flavour of Walkers crisps. I can almost guarantee you won't see Gary Lineker advertising minge and muff flavour crisps whilst exclaiming "It tastes just like the real thing!" any time soon.

However, Charlotte did ponder what flavour she should state that her lady love tasted like. The options seemed endless: prawn cocktail, salt and vinegar and cheese and onion all came to mind. *Nope,* she thought as she looked at her half-eaten lunch, *my vagina shall taste of scrambled eggs and coleslaw* she self-declared with a potentially misplaced sense of pride.

To be fair to this knob... I mean man, he was not enticed with this particularly dire combination of vaginal flavours. I am not convinced that is overly the greatest of compliments. It is somewhat like praising my child for missing a square inch of the wall when they have redecorated the rest of the lounge as an impromptu stick figure art gallery. Essentially, the damage has still been done, but it has been marginally minimalised. Nonetheless, I feel obliged to salute Tobias, as some internet weirdos would have asked for some brown sauce on the side. I will leave your imagination to decipher what that could mean because, to be perfectly honest, the authorship of this book has scarred me enough already.

Charlotte was disappointed that her flavoured vulva did not seem to titillate Tobias so she endeavoured to persuade him otherwise. The following should read in the voice of Joey in the little-known US sitcom *Friends* when he is describing Rachel's meat trifle fiasco: "What's not to like? Scrambled eggs, good. Coleslaw, good!"

Success! Tobias had uncovered his inner Heston Blumenthal and now was finally onboard with Charlotte's unusually flavoured poontang pie. Tobias, with his new found love of genitalia gastronomy, claimed that his shaft tasted like cheese and pickle. Admittedly the taste of cheese could be from a lack of cleanliness but this was sad news for Charlotte to hear nonetheless. Unfortunately, for this budding relationship between these two sexual foodies, Charlotte was rather severely dairy intolerant. Therefore, the most likely outcome from intercourse between these two would be an unsettled stomach and a potential shart.

A Festive Foot Job

It is Christmas time and we all are having some fun...oh God, not that much fun! Put that away Jerome, you filthy little bastard. Here we are at Christmas. I do realise I am writing this in June but the mind of a true author has no limitations in imagination. The nuts are roasting, the turkey is stuffed, the sack is bulging and the stockings are bursting at the seams. Wow! Christmas is an innuendo minefield, isn't it? I feel this innuendo infestation needs to be researched.

The website www.EliteDaily.com has us covered with 'bedroom talk' that will be full of 'Christmas cheer' and as 'hot as some mulled wine'. 6 Start that cold shower now because we are about to heat this tale up with some sexual puns which are sure to stoke the fire within your pants. Some of the puns listed are undeniably obvious, for instance, 'cumming down your chimney tonight'. 7 As a health-related side note, it is essential to remember that, if one chooses to cum down a chimney without the correct safety gear, it is important to always use a chimney sweep to avoid unwanted soot babies.

I cannot imagine a man being thrilled with the next festive bedroom talk as it seems to insinuate that they are less than well endowed. If I heard the phrase 'Santa needs a little helper' come out from the mouth of a lover I would immediately get dressed and cry into some tinsel at my miniaturised manhood. 8 There was another pun that sounded rather painful for the male participant. 'I'll be a real nutcracker' Elite Daily suggested with a certain amount of whimsy. 9 I have no idea what a fake sexual nutcracker is, let alone what a real one would entail. However, the idea of my testicles being crushed until they crack does not fill me with any amount of yuletide lust.

There are some that make no sense whatsoever, for instance, 'Jack Frost's nipples on your nose' to which even the author comments 'eh?'. 10 I for one have never desired a nipple to be dragged like a fleshy stylus across my nose let alone the nipple of a man who is notoriously ice cold. Lastly, and most oddly, 'I'm going to ride you like a reindeer' is a rather disturbing suggestion that edges on the realm of bestiality. 11

I refuse to search 'reindeer sex' to find out what this would entail. There is a line I shall not cross for this book and, as it turns out, watching Rudolph going balls deep in Donner is it. As an educated assumption, I presume a human re-enactment of reindeer sex would be the man adorning a twig on his head whilst violently thrusting his furry penis into a woman on all fours as she bleats for the whole two minutes the intercourse lasts. Does that not sound romantic and festive? Well, with all that said, I hope I have brought you some 'Christmas cheer' and we can continue with the story of Stephanie.

Let's be frank here for one moment, (you can be Claudia or Stuart if you please) the tinsel, presents, turkey, stockings, crackers, tree and the sweet baby Jesus feign in comparison to what is the ultimate Christmas symbol: the holy foot job. Yeah, I said it. We were all thinking it but I am obviously the only one brave enough to say it aloud. The foot job is the quintessential Christmas pastime that all of us can enjoy over the festive period. Wait one second, I am being informed by my editor this is not true? Well, jingle my bells and baste my ball sack this is news to me and it will most certainly be news to Terrence.

Stephanie had written she liked to play a bit of footsie on her online bio. To reiterate, she did not write she liked anal, threesomes, electric shocks to the nipples or pegging, but merely the rather innocent act of flirtatiously stroking someone's foot. As it turned out this was a rather massive mistake. For it is written on the internet (somewhere) that, if one broadcasts a desire to stroke feet, then one is a sex obsessed maniac who would like endless sexual invitations from random men. Don't blame me for this, I did not write the online handbook.

Terrence was an inquisitive soul. Scratch that Terrence was a perverted soul. He saw the utterance of footsie on Stephanie's bio and thought, *Well then, now this woman does indeed want to suckle my tootsies like a pair of pigs in blankets*. As a side note, I legitimately felt a bit sick writing that last bit. Regardless, with Christmas fast approaching like an oncoming freight train, Terrence had a matter of utter most importance to query Stephanie about. Terrence typed with his smegma and Cheeto stained fingers "Are foot fondles allowed at the Christmas dinner table?"

With a wit as sharp and quick as a vaccination, Stephanie retorted "I am sorry but I am more a stuffing kind of girl." I mean this is entirely understandable, at our local carvery I would quite contently have a whole plate of stuffing and forget the meat, potatoes and carrots entirely. You heard me, I said screw the meat and two vegetables. That may have possibly been a really poor selection of words, my apologies.

Well Terrence was not best pleased with this and instead he insisted "I wanted you to rub my cock at the table whilst we eat our roast." Let me set this scene for you reader. Grab a pillow, get snuggled under a blanket and listen to this fictional scenario. Wait one second Janet, these are actual instructions. The narrative will not continue until these criteria are met. Paul, I can see your foot poking out of the cover. Attaboy, that is better. Right, we may now continue.

The entire family are gathered around the table. I am not just talking about immediate family here, but also the ones who would be unrecognisable if it wasn't for the pictures of them in that dusty old photo album in the loft. 98-year-old Nana Pat has travelled down from an undisclosed location known only as 'up North' looking like an anorexic skeleton. She may very well be a White Walker (note to self to check if the gravy boat is made from dragon glass).

The umpteenth argument of the day had erupted because Auntie Cheryl mentioned that one time when Auntie Gwen had sex with Dashing Darren from school when she knew she was 'totally in love with him'. Uncle Steve sits there sullen, staring longingly at the carving knife wondering if today will be the day he snaps. Meanwhile, his wife, the aforementioned Cheryl, is now necking shots of mulled wine like it was a night out in Ibiza. Mum brings out the roast potatoes, which look mysteriously like the coal that Santa delivers to the naughty children, whilst

Dad gloats over the new turkey recipe that makes the poultry behemoth at the centre of the table taste at least one per cent less dry and like reconstructed cardboard.

In walks Stephanie, but oh what is this?... she has a new man. *Well, isn't that wonderful,* we all think simultaneously. She is such a lovely girl, the real treasure of this sunken ship of a family. She can do no wrong, she is angelic, perfection incarnated and what is more now she has an equally wonderful man in her life. Stephanie sits down with her other half and the table grows silent in anticipation for the introduction of 'the man'.

"Hey everyone. Hey Great Nana Pat, why are your eyes glowing blue? Never mind... this is.... ummm... well this is Terrence".

Terrence what an old school name. The name of a true gentlemen, the collective consciousness of the table thinks.

"Terrence likes my feet..."

Well, someone better because those talons look like they could carry off a small child, thinks Nana Pat to herself.

"He likes them so much I might toss him off under the table later with them, but I will be really discrete, I promise. He has already said he won't make the orgasm face, haven't you dear? I hope that is okay with everyone? Oh, and we brought some bread sauce for everyone to share. It's Terrence's secret recipe. Love you, Nana."

Cut to next year's Christmas dinner and the umpteenth argument has erupted because Stephanie, now single, has been reminded of the time that her date's ejaculate launched across the table onto the plate of Nana Pat who unknowingly ate it with her trifle.

Back to the real-life Terrence who is still centred on the idea of footsie. He states, with a matter of urgency that seems disproportionate to the content of his words, "All that matters is that I will beat you at footsies." I do apologise for the insensitive nature of the following statement Terrence; however, I highly doubt the leading scientists of the world are going to halt their research into the cure for cancer because the latest results of Division Two of The Footsie League have shaken the sport to its very core.

Nonetheless, Terrence insists that, with his victory, Stephanie will be forced to admit her undying love for him. Yeah... because that was definitely the one factor that was holding her back from you, a foot obsessed, total stranger. Your ability to stroke a foot was most definitely the looming question mark over this potential romance.

One could argue that, if the main source of compliments you receive from other human beings is that you are a fantastic footsie player, then you may need to invest in a personality or a hobby. With a sense of determination, only found in the most avid of sociopaths, he continued "My footsie is inevitable." This sounds like a threat from the world's worst super villain ever created. Seriously, Stan Lee or Jack Kirby must have been really scraping the bottom of the barrel for this one. *The Avengers* will surely meet their ultimate match attempting to take down The Footsie Fetish Fiend. After all, I have heard Captain America has extremely sensitive inner thighs.

The next tangent of this conversation caught Stephanie, and me for that matter, somewhat off guard. "Do you think you could crush me if you wrapped your legs around me and squeezed me like an anaconda?"

"That is incredibly specific. It is also incredibly unlikely," replied Stephanie with a grin "Because that would mean I would want to be near you."

"I am sure the pain would be worth it," he wrote, somehow still unrelentless. Stephanie thought to herself, I *am sure it would be, but so would putting your pencil dick in a meat grinder. I mean admittedly not worth it for yourself, but me and the rest of the female gender, would have a right giggle.*

Before ending this tale, I would like to note Francis's brief tale, as it also features a footsie fiend. Francis was an avid amateur dancer. This was of immense concern to Steve. He was concerned that his footsie abilities would result in her premature retirement from her beloved passion. He elaborated that the male gender is notoriously clumsy, which let's be honest is entirely true. However, how the fuck clumsy can one possibly be? I have dyspraxia, so therefore I am naturally clumsier than most. I mean I have been known to accidentally smash a plate, or spill a drink on the floor, but not once have I accidentally shoved my foot into someone's vagina during a mere game of footsie. Have I been doing it wrong? Is that the end goal? It is becoming more apparent why my previous relationships have not worked out.

Steve reassured Francis that this was not a cause for concern as there was a lot more to do under a table than footsie. He claimed he would be able to convince Francis to wear a short skirt to a meal out and then the real fun would begin. Francis simply exclaimed "how the absolute fuck would you convince me to wear a short skirt? It is the middle of Winter, if you have not noticed. It is fucking freezing outside. My fufu would look like an artic cave with icicles precariously dangling down from it." Steve conceded this was a flaw, however, he expressed a desire to run his fingers up and down Francis's legs to which Francis said, startled, "I wouldn't mate. I am hairy as fuck right now. A proper Covid lockdown Muffalo." I think Steve may have noted Francis's lack of interest, or possibly he was too scared to continue this romantic endeavour, after finding out that the Muffalo's favourite food was scrambled Steve.

(A Not So) Blast from the Past

For most of us, our childhoods are often the easiest, least stressful and best times of our lives filled with fun, laughter and joy. Obviously, there are some exceptions to this claim; for starters the children of Westeros have to deal with disease, murder, assault, the death of loved ones, ice zombies, homicidal royalty and mother fucking dragons to name but a few hindrances to their childhood.

Nonetheless, for those that do not live in a magical dark age, we tend to view this time of our lives with rose tinted glasses. It seems, to our adult selves, that our childhood world was immaculate and flawless. This tinted view causes us to see the differences that the modern era has instilled into our lives, as an assault on our perfect childhood.

One such modern interference is the rise of the internet and its subsequent takeover of every aspect of our lives. It has been accused of a multitude of heinous crimes against society; from the devolution of communication, the rise of an obesity pandemic and, most unforgivable of all, the fame of the YouTuber *Blippi*. However, one area that most would agree has been affected negatively, is the world of dating. These negative aspects can be seen within these very pages from catfishing to the over prioritisation of looks. Most individuals from that era would claim that the old means to date far outmatches the modern tech-based form of now.

Let me counter that notion with a question... but was it really? Come one now, let's all have a real hard think about that one. To aid with the answer, let me take you on journey back in time to the year of 1999. So, put down your Nintendo 64 controller, strap on your pair of roller-skates and head to the local internet café to explore Susan's tale with me. The world was on the cusp of a new millennium. Britney Spears was dominating the charts, *The Matrix* was defining a generation of cinema and Susan was of the innocent age of 18.

Susan did not have a means to scour the internet for suitors like us modern folk do, but instead relied on her friends to match her with blind dates.

When her best friend, Amanda, went on a first date, she would take Susan with her and therefore, make it a double date. Susan's match would usually be found from within the confines of the local zoo or asylum, by her friend Amanda's date. This is where the crux of this tale emerges its ugly head.

It was the 90's, so of course Susan donned her best halter neck top and zebra print pencil skirt and waited patiently outside her work for her Romeo. A flashy Mercedes arrived. The kind of car that made everyone who laid eyes on it know that whoever was inside was incredibly important. I arrive in a bus, take from that what you will.

Who could it be? Romantic images of Leonardo DiCaprio flinging the doors open and whisking her into his arms before drawing her, like one of his French girls, flooded her mind. However, alas it was not Leonardo DiCaprio, nor Tom Cruise, Will Smith or any other 90's heartthrob. No, instead from within this luxurious automobile, came her date like a bulldozer to her heart.

The man who towered above her at a colossal 6ft 9in was clad head to toe in leather with a Stetson adorning his head. Susan was unaware that the term 'blind date', in fact, referred to her date's insistence to select his outfit blindfolded in the dark. The result was this bizarre costume choice before her that looked like a cross between a member of *The Vengaboys* and an eccentric cowboy. This outfit was not even practical as wild west attire, as the wearer would sweat and chafe in the hot desert sun more than a certain disgraced royal family member at a school disco. Let's all be honest here, for a man who claims he cannot sweat, his head sure sweated a lot in that infamous interview.

Oh, I should most probably interject here and explain who the *Vengaboys* were to the younger folk. First of all, the band's choices in costume often looked like they were sponsored by both a low budget Halloween fancy-dress shop and a seedy sex store, both of whom wanted their clothes line to be on show the most. As for their music career, well for a brief moment, try to remember a ridiculously cheesy pop song you have heard at a wedding, party or even school disco. The likelihood is that it was the *Vengaboys*.

Their hits are undeniably lyrically complex, full of deep meaning, conceits and hidden symbolism. For instance, the repetition of the word 'boom' in their hit song title is not, as one would most certainly believe, about a firework display. However, as one line reveals it is in fact about a woman simply describing her desire to have sex with a man in her room. Likewise, the narrative of the track *We Like To Party* is not the anti-war and fascism arc most assume, but instead it is meant to reinforce the love that the band has for partying. I know, rest now, for thy mind has been blown with the sheer brilliance and wonder of the *Vengaboys*.

Now that we are all on an even playing field in terms of *Vengaboys* knowledge, let us commence. Susan sat in the luxurious car, for lack of better words, fucked off. I was not in the car at the time as I was seven and, therefore, was not allowed to be out after 5pm. Nonetheless, I believe I can take an educated estimation at what Susan's scornful face translated to, which was, *Amanda, if we were not the closest of friends, I would inflict unimaginable pain upon you right now you absolute cum guzzler*. Meanwhile, her friend's face seemed to convey a mixture of shock, horror and unmistakable guilt which when combined said, *please, have mercy on me*. Susan's date presumably was blissfully unaware of the unspoken argument that was happening within the confines of his car. Instead, in my mind at least, he was shooting his finger pistols into the air whilst performing a rendition of *We're Going to Ibiza*.

Unfortunately, the car was not en route to Ibiza, nor any other summer time getaway where Brian from down the road could bronze his man titties without fear of ridicule. They were, instead, headed to her date's home so he could get changed into something a bit more fitting for the occasion. *Thank actual fuck for that*, thought Susan, *he might actually be putting on a shirt and look less like Lurch from the Addams Family in a gimp suit.*

Oh dear, fuck, Susan internally sighed as her date presented himself in his 'change' of clothes. The word 'change' may have been a tad of an over exaggeration on his part, it was more of a mere palette swap. He stood there in front of her in the exact same outfit but with one key difference, the whole damn thing was now purple. It seemed, like all the best *Vengaboys* action figures, his outfit apparently came in a multitude of colours to suit almost any occasion, including his own murder at the hands of an ever increasingly unamused blind date.

Barney, the leather clad dinosaur, then started what can only be described as the oddest game of Simon Says in human   existence.   Let's   play   along,   shall   we? "Simon says, stand-up."

Well, this seems like rather standard fare so far... there seems to be no cause for concern. Activate: standing up.

"Simon says, do a twirl."

Well, to be honest this seems fine. I will act like the beautiful ballerina I am and do said twirl.

"Suck that strangers dick for £30 for me, will you sweet cheeks?"

"Aha, you didn't say Simon says," I say as I brush the dirt from my knees and zip said stranger's flies back up before sending him on his merry way.

 Yes, as it turns out all was not as it seemed with Susan's date. It seemed bad to start with so for it to be worse is a rather impressive feat. After Susan's demonstration of her exceptional twirling capabilities, Barney declared that she 'would do' and could 'earn him a lot of money'. Yes, for those more innocent readers, Barney was indeed a pimp. It is no wonder he had a friend called BJ on the classic children's TV show. In fact, I am officially changing his nickname to suit his new purple pimp style, to Willy Wanka.

Amanda and Susan finally arrived in town and started a frantic search for a means of escape from their potential future employer. A bathroom beckoned to them as salvation and from here these two near women of the streets fled into the safety of the night. Understandably, after an evening where she had been nearly loaned out for sex as a prostitute, it was safe to say that Susan never trusted Amanda with a double date again. So, were the good ol' days of dating better than the modern, tech infested means of now? No, as it turns out both are absolute shit.

Dick Down

I feel old. No, not because of the ball sack that doth descend to street level, nor because bending down to pick up my packet of Werther's originals has now become a feat of unimaginable bravery laced with danger. To be honest, I cannot remember where I last parked the car, let alone where I left the keys.

The music charts are full of indecipherable ramblings and noise, whilst the television is full of knobheads desperate for fame. Whilst these are all true, the real reason I know I am now officially old is because I have no damn clue about what the fuck a lot of twentysomethings are saying.

Feeling lost in translation will be an issue for most when one first starts to match on their chosen online dating platform. You will be bombarded by acronyms that seem like a mere jumble of letters and words that sound like they originated from a fantasy world. To emphasise this point it is time for a quick pop quiz. Below is a list of legitimate modern acronyms about sex: 1. DTR 2. CU46 3. WTTP 4. DTF 5. TDTM 6. RUH 7. CIM 8. ATM 9. GNOC 10. DDF 12

Confused? Me too. When I first went online to find a match, I was afraid that I would launch a nuclear strike on Bognor Regis due to my lack of knowledge about internet slang. Fortunately for me, and the population of Bognor

Regis, a swift search of Google will deliver the meaning behind the letters. I have written the answers to the above test in the endnotes as to avoid cheating. If you scored:

0-3 - Congratulations! You are a literate, intelligent human being.

4-6 - This is not your first rodeo in the online dating world, and you have already endured the devolution of human language.

7-10 - You are part of the problem. Pick up a dictionary and learn some real words. Sorry, that must have made no sense. Yo my homeboy, scoop up a dictionizzle and bone up on some chatter.

Now, with that rant over, I can attempt to tackle Hannah's tale. Hannah was having a streak of bad luck with men. All of them thus far seemed to be assholes, perverts, sexists, racists or a combination of the above. Oh, who is that metaphorically knock knocking on Hannah's phone screen? It is Alan, the little scoundrel. He would like to 'dick down'. *Hmmm,* Hannah considered *potentially, Alan has made a grammatical error and he, instead, meant Richard...also known as Dick, his veteran brother in arms, who was killed in action i.e., is down*. Potentially, Hannah had intercepted a top-secret military comms via a dating app where a distraught soldier confirmed the death of his comrade (a Saving Private Dick, if you will). However, that seemed a bit farfetched. Could it be that he was talking to his own genitals and asking as to why they were flaccid rather than being stood at attention for the spectacle of the woman in front of him? This also seemed also unlikely.

"Well then, I am not sure what the fuck that means to be honest," Hannah shouted defeated. "Alexa, what does dick down mean?" Hannah asks her AI companion out of desperation.

"I'd rather not answer that," Alexa retorts in a somewhat judgemental tone.

"What a load of shit this robot is. Turns out *Wall-E* was a complete lie. Not only are robots not cute but they are also fucking useless," she said angrily at the inanimate object. "Well, hopefully Google isn't such a prude and will help me." Google was also a prude.

"I might as well ask him then and face the embarrassment of not being down with the kids," Hannah said with a sadness that reflected her realisation she was old.

"Yo, homie."

Before we delve further into this conversation, I would like to mention that Microsoft Word thinks I am an absolute illiterate twat and has underlined most of the words that follow.

"You hear me, love. Dick down is all the craze. I dicked down with Francessca and Sharon last week. You feel me, sweet?"

Oh, dear fuck this hurts to write. I apologise Hannah, carry on. Hannah even more confused asked "But what does it mean?"

"Ah shit, you feel me? I will spell it out for you. [I am confident spelling is not this man's forte] It means a dick going in and of your vagina really fast and intense like."

"Oh," Hannah states as she starts to process this information "You mean sex. Normal... sex."

"Yeah, little Miss, you down for it?"

"I do apologise for not understanding, but I was too busy cooky wooky my dindans whilst televisually ogling *Bake Off*. What makes 'dick down so intense?"

"Eh? You an odd one. You see, it is the best cause you will be moaning in my ear," he announced.

Hannah realised that the only thing she would most likely be moaning about with this man is his evident lack of grasp of the English language. The other option is that he meant Hannah would be constantly moaning about the dirty dishes. Most likely that little fucker would be fiddily diddling his dicky up whilst no one does the washy uppy the dishy wishies. With this in mind, and without the imminent aid of a translator, Hannah decided to terminate the conversation. Unfortunately for him his dick would not be going down, nor up, nor left, nor right in her vicinity in the future.

Knock, Knock You're Blocked

I like to think I am rather humorous to some extent. I tend to at least make those around me, without the threat of violence no less, chuckle. To be fair, this could be a case of nervous laughter. The kind similar to when Nana Mildred tells a 'hilarious' anecdote about the time she once was involved in a bukkake session with ten or twelve men. It is a laughter, mixed with sheer fear, intertwined with awkwardness.

To be honest, this book could contradict the notion that I am hilarious. It could reveal the terrifying truth that I am in a fact a mere man sat in boxer shorts who rants absolute rubbish to an audience of sympathetic Samaritans whom have taken pity on me. However, I will state this, I am a lot funnier than the wannabe failed comedians in the next tale.

A joke. It seems like a concrete means to break the ice and initiate conversation with a member of the opposite sex. That is correct, my astute fellow (or mam, or whatever you may identify yourself as). However, to be able to write these hilarious one-liners, one must undergo years of training and in my case, a marital separation and mental breakdown, though I do not believe these to be mandatory. To summarise, it is hard to be funny. I am not suggesting it is the hardest occupation. No, in fact I would argue, to some surprisingly, that performing lifesaving surgery is considerably more complex than writing a funny. However, please do feel free to disagree with that comment and instead worship my plight against the many hardships of writing such anecdotes as cousin Matilda and the unfortunate cucumber incident.

Nonetheless, humour does not seem a natural stone for some individuals to step on. Whilst a one-liner can be a fantastic ice breaker it can also, if mishandled, sink a conversation like a lead balloon attached to the Titanic. The following is an example of one hell of an awful one liner; a demonstration of a joke that did not so much attract a partner but make them run for the hills instead.

It should be obvious not to be racist. As obvious as the knowledge that smearing honey over oneself and leaping into a bear enclosure does not constitute a clever idea. As a sound, functional and decent member of the human race, this disdain for racism should be second nature. However, there are still a few proverbial stains on the blanket that is human existence and that, despite excessive scrubbing, refuse to come out.

I remember a while ago; I was walking down the street living the gangster-in-paradise-esque lifestyle I do find myself in. The street was bustling, well for my small town it was at least. To be perfectly honest there was about three people, a pigeon and a dog. So, the street was alive. A pleasant sound burst into my eardrum like a firework of symphonies; the sound of a busker playing her saxophone.

She was talented for sure, though I may not be the best judge of musical ability. I am no Simon Cowell after all. I tend to shout loudly rather than sing harmoniously in the shower. Nonetheless, I was transfixed and in awe.

Then, out of the musical euphoria, erupted a woman like a fart in an orchestra. She had a hunched back, teeth befitting of a beaver and a neck that looked like my Grandad's ball sack. To be perfectly honest my disdain for her may be colouring in her physical profile with a shitty crayon somewhat. I feel, deep down, that she may just be a standard old woman.

She slithered on her belly towards me (there goes that disdain again) and asked "Do you know if she is a foreigner?" pointing towards said busker with her talons. I looked confused and looked down. No, I was not accidentally wearing my *UK Border Force* fancy dress costume from the epic 'shit television' themed 2018 Halloween party again.

I simply replied "Sorry, I do not know," and added internally, *Why the fuck would I?*

She contorted herself towards the busker, her arms and legs dislocating, as she scurried towards her prey. A brief conversation passed and then she scuttled back to me "Nah, she's foreign! I am not giving her any money." Now, colour me confused because, does the fact she is a 'foreigner' mean her talent becomes mute and your enjoyment of her wonderful music vanishes. I feel sorry for this woman who must live a rather sad, shallow and pathetic life without much musical joy and wonder. Has she never got down and funky to *ABBA's Dancing Queen'*? Or has she never mellowed out to *Bob Marley's One Love'*?

Does this also mean that she has never rocked out to *Motörhead's Ace of Spades*? I, for one, appreciate talent no matter it's source. I shoved a fiver into the busker's pot and applauded her talent right in front of Freddy Kruger's Nan's racist, wrinkled ass face.

I don't understand racism. I mean, I cannot fathom or tolerate it at all. It makes no sense. The notion that the colour of one's skin can create such hatred baffles me, more so than the adoration that children have for the hallucinogenic hellscape that is *In the Night Garden*. Skin colour is a trait we are born with. It is decided via the chemical reaction that denotes the amount of melanin our bodies create and therefore, it cannot be chosen. In contrast, I can decide to not be a fat fuck, but here I am about to consume a Mars bar. You can hate me but at least I will have chocolate.

I have a friend called Thomas. He has enormous ears. He is aware of this, as is the rest of the world. I, and no one I have met, hate him for this. Nor do I hate the woman down the road with the crooked nose. Well at least not for her crooked nose. That woman once invited the entire street to her house for a BBQ other than me and my children. Neither do I hate those with a flat chest, brown eyes, outward bellybuttons, blonde hair, those who are left-handed or have dyslexia. I do not hate them because these were not choices. These were traits that were genetically transferred to them. I do hate, however, those who dislike another for their race, because that is a choice. You have chosen to be an absolute dickhead.

To summarise for us decent folk, the notion of racism is most likely one of the most undesirable traits in a potential love interest, unless white robes and ridiculous pointy hats are a turn on for you. Therefore, it is safe to assume that a racist one liner would float no one's boat. The cretin of this tale, Frank, did not receive this memo. In fact, Frank did not seem to receive mail at all. This is because Frank is a friendless, racist knob. Not one of those nice knobs either, not the kind that is welcomed with the enthusiasm of an over excitable feral rabbit into the front and back avenues of The Divorced Dad Street. No, instead he is a knob that should be taken to a lab and studied via dissection to understand his extreme tendencies towards awfulness.

Frank, the anal lick he is, sent a woman named Janine an offensive and insensitive one liner that was also racist. Here lies an issue with this tale. The standard structure so far has been as follows: I paraphrase and over-exaggerate what the sexual deviants of these tales have said. Then with expert skill, impeccable wit and flawless cunning I tear these assholes a new one. However, I would rather not waste the word count or time on the words this abhorrent wanker spoke.

"But, uh why? Why is racism a turn off? I just don't get it." asks Frank dumbfounded as he itches his bum and sniffs the brown rainbow from within. Well, you most fragrant of farts, lets imagine an existence that is devoid of ass hats like yourself. An absolute absurd, and unprofitable for me, proposition, I know. Who else would the tales of this book be based on? This book would have less content than my last attempt at writing a novel 'The Many Perks of Keeping a Pet Ant'. That was one community I did not expect to offend...the ant farm owners of this world will be absolutely fuming.

In this utopian alternative universe, we all live in peace and harmony despite our differences in sexuality, race, religion or beliefs. The definition of heaven on Earth. Hark here comes Frank to ruin our bliss with an absolute belter of racial rudeness to revolt the ears of the innocent. It seems that most individuals neither support, nor condone these horrendous beliefs that plague our world. In fact, one could argue they would be found rather outrageously offensive and reflect badly on an individual's character. You could essentially pull down your pants, sit on the kitchen floor and then scoot along the tiles butt naked leaving a shitty trail in your wake. Even after all that you, in many ways, would still be considered more attractive than a racist.

It seems Frank has not listened; he is too preoccupied with picking the sweetcorn out from under his nails from a particular in depth delve into his anal cavity. Let's continue in the foolish belief that these words could sink into his thick skull. Imagine for a moment you meet your dream woman. Though in Frank's case I am not entirely convinced he is human... so, dream female Slurpon from the planet Slush (don't ask, I have no idea why slushies are on my mind).

You obviously want to make the best first impression and as it just happens you have the perfect joke to really tickle her funny bone and woo her. The lads down at the conservative club find it hilarious after all, so of course she will too. The drum rolls and boom. That overly offensive, sure to be hit of a one liner is sent. However, how does one know that this woman, or Slurpon in Frank's case, does not have friends, relatives or loved ones who are potentially trans, gay or another ethnicity? You simply don't. In the modern era, it is incredibly likely, in fact, that she knows someone who is a part of a marginalised community. Congratulations, you moron. You have, through sheer ignorance, isolated and upset a potential love interest, you utter twat.

Baggage Claims

Food. It is an undeniable bliss, albeit one that causes one's stomach to increase in size and look like a deflated balloon or at least, that is what happens to me. Unless one lives with a Michelin star chef, a restaurant is most likely the most effective means to consume the best food the world has to offer. However, it is without a shadow of doubt, the entire restaurant experience that determines the overall quality and satisfaction of a meal. Even if the food makes one drool like Auntie Shannon when the final number is called at the bingo hall and she is one number from a full house, it can be hampered with the discovery of a stray pube. Likewise, noise level, bad table service, lacklustre health standards, awful food or a ridiculous wait can also be detrimental to the restaurant experience. However, I think one factor can truly make or break a meal: the company.

"Bonjour," said the waiter at the Italian restaurant, which seemed odd due to the fact that was an obvious French welcome. Aria's French had, like for most of us, not been used since the forced lessons at school. However, she did know what 'hello' was and also a choice few curse words, though these French profanities do not seem relevant to this tale. Nonetheless, somewhat baffled about the waiter's evident cuisine confusion, Aria walked into the restaurant. She was welcomed with an empty seat at her table. A seat that remained empty for a total of 42 minutes. That is 2520 seconds. That is almost an entire half of a football match.

At 12 minutes, that is 720 seconds for those who choose to measure time in seconds, she decided to text her man. 'I've been here for 10 minutes. Are you still coming?'

'Yes, on my way,' came the no nonsense reply at a time when 'nonsense' would have been very much appreciated. At 24 minutes, or 1200 seconds, Aria left the table to relieve herself in the facilities, a fantastic metaphor for this whole evening. This date was truly going down the toilet or, to be blunt, in the shitter. 2100 seconds in, (I will leave the minutes as a math calculation for those who feel inclined), it was time for Aria to leave. She said her farewells to the staff who had chatted and looked after her whilst she waited. She settled the bill, which consisted of the bulk of the cocktail menu (it was so worth it) and entered the cool late afternoon air. Her mobile buzzed in her coat 'I am a minute from the restaurant. Wait for me.' said an authoritative voice.

Against her better judgement, Aria waited. Her date arrived. He was handsome, athletic and wore a nice black suit. For all his faults, he was at least pleasant to look at. However, he did not excuse himself for his tardiness, but instead rushed them into the restaurant. His first real act of 'romance' was to moan that Aria had allowed him to come into the restaurant with his Bluetooth headset still shoved into his ear. I mean it is arguable, to most reasonable people at least, that one should be in charge of the objects found in their own orifices. I have yet to have the audacity to shout at my girlfriend for forgetting to tell me to remove the butt plug from my anus when watching a film at the local cinema. That was one hell of an uncomfortable 9 hours and 17 minutes, or 33,420 seconds, of watching *The Lord of the Rings Trilogy* with Sergeant Stoppage embedded into my asshole.

The turn of conversation was not much better. It involved an extensive TED talk about his ex-wife. He was not a fan. He called her all the names under the Sun, and potentially Mars and even Venus. She had left him for another man and now lived down the road from him. She had also had a child with her current other half, or as he called the innocent infant, an 'it'.

Let's pause for one second here. I need to vent. So, I am The Divorced Dad. This means me and my ex-wife are no more. In other words; the flames of that love died out, the car that is our marriage ran out of fuel or our Happy Meal of romance became happy-less. Whatever metaphor we choose to acknowledge the fact is, regrettably, that relationship is over. Is it sad? Yes. Did it hurt? Yes. Did I shed tears? Hell yeah. Was I mad? For a brief moment, I indeed was.

So, in the initial research for The Divorced Dad, I scoured Facebook for groups and pages that referenced divorced dads. Wow, is that a kettle of fish that smelt of a pungent, anti-Mum sentiment. Men who seemed to hate women who had birthed children, especially their own.   I understand the anger, pain and frustration to some degree. There are incredible men out there who have had suffered unbelievable injustices. Some have had everything snatched from their arms in an instance at the hands of a divorce.

It is undeniable that father rights are an area of contention and immeasurable pain.   Inarguably, I speak from the relative safety of a genuine friendship with my ex and non-restrictive access to my children. I still cannot fathom the hate that some individuals, with full access to their children, have towards their exes. For some, it seems the emotion of hate arises because it is what is expected from them. Society says we should feel resentment for those who hurt us, so we do without question. But why? Yes, the relationship deteriorated but surely, it is possible to scrape a friendship from the ruins of love, even if it is wholly for the benefit of our children. After all, the effort needed to hate is both immense and tiring.

It could be the case that men have been told for generations that sadness is a sign of weakness. The idea of the macho man has been embedded into our culture as the desired model of manliness. After all, how can you be the breadwinner and protector of your family if you feel like crying when the will of the world is unfair to you? So, instead of becoming emotional, some men instinctually turn to anger when presented with an event that is upsetting or difficult to process. Could it be that these men who 'hate' their ex-lovers are in reality heartbroken and unable to communicate their loss?

The man in front of Aria continued to vent about his ex, either in denial about his heart break or an utter tosser. No matter the reason, Aria decided to end the date after an hour and a half of torturous conversation. She walked outside with her wannabe lover, her mind racing to find a polite excuse to turn down a second date. He turned to her and muttered under his breath "Let's not bother with a second date, you have a bit too much baggage for me."

Excuse me one second, Mr. Ex-Wife Hater, what the actual fuck?

As it turns out the French curse words are relevant to this tale as Aria screamed "va te faire enculer!", the translation I will leave for you to decipher.

Rich Uncle Pennybags

Fun fact: Rich Uncle Pennybags is the real name of the moustached, suited, top hat wearing mascot of Monopoly.

I like to believe this book has attracted an audience that is open-minded, understanding, compassionate and has a modern outlook on the world. With that said, if we are truly understanding we must accept the world of kinks and fetishes. Womans Health stated in 2016 that 1 in 6 individuals have a fetish and what is more 1 in 3 have tried a kink at least once. 13 With over 549 Paraphilia's acknowledged by researchers and 'mainstream' sex openly becoming more adventurous, it feels like we may need to start to acknowledge and accept this element of sex. 14

The next individual, let's name him Grant, has no issue whatsoever with the more unusual side of intercourse. His first message to Lauren was not a courteous 'hello there,' nor a 'how are you doing?', but instead was a sexual statement of intent. It read as follows: 'I am into the following: 1. Rimming 2. Licking a lass out 3. Licking and sucking feet 4. Rough dominating fucking 5. Adventurous fucking.'

There are a few important details within this list to examine. Firstly, the consistent use of the term 'fucking' instead of 'sex', or another plausible synonym is unusual.

I have had sex, sure. I know check me out, although how baffles me on a daily basis to be honest. However, I have not once, to my knowledge, had a fucking. In this context, it sounds weird and infantile, yet somehow also geriatric.

I mean what is 'adventurous fucking'? Is it a role-play where the man puts on a fedora, does his best Harrison Ford impression and attempts to find hidden artefacts that are buried within a vagina? A womb raider, if you will. I feel the aforementioned statement needs to be more defined. One person's adventurous is another's meh and vice versa, one person's meh can be another person's "get that the fuck out of there." Adventure is a wide field even in film. To my son, *Dora the Explorer* is a high-octane adventure that is full of adrenaline and wonder. To me however, it is about a lonely, sad Spanish girl who has some form of mental issue and hallucinates make believe scenarios to fill the dark void in her life. To be fair, he finds *Star Wars* utter horse shite, so I think we are about even in the appreciation of each other's cinematic tastes.

I also am hesitant to suggest it would be a worthwhile endeavour to find out whether your match is at all sexually adventurous before unloading your horny shopping list onto them, the items of which can only be found in the 'from behind' aisle in Lidl. Lauren was not adventurous. I mean she had tried kink before and it was not for her at all. She was a self-confessed lover of 'vanilla' flavour sex. After all, we cannot all be lovers of chocolate, cat food and soy sauce flavoured sex, can we? To make this clear in the nicest of manners, she stated that she would rather play a three-hour marathon game of Monopoly than participate in option 1 through 5.

Grant, either blissfully unaware or ignorantly determined, exclaims "I can be the board." Now, let's examine the practicalities of this set up, shall we? For starters, this 'board', as so lovingly shown off in your profile picture of you topless holding your 'catch of the day', is evidently not a flat surface, so traversing said board could be an issue.   What is more, I would not want to lose my tiny, metallic hat within a fold, crack, or crevice when attempting to purchase Bond Street which has suddenly been relocated to near your naval. I can only imagine the owners of the luxurious establishments scattered across said street were rather confused and irritated when their storefronts now overlooked your fleshy Grand Canyon that smelt of rotted Quavers.

Finally, the important question of where do I shove my playing piece when I am forced into jail? And, therefore subsequently, will you be happy with a metal kitten lodged up your butthole for the maximum penalty of three rounds?   In fact, given your preference for adventurous sex, I probably would not like to know the answer to those questions.

Lauren declined the human board game experience that was so enthusiastically offered to her by Rich Uncle Moneybags. Instead, she decided to announce to her match that she, in fact, was not fond of sex at all. Was this knobhead deterred? Like fuck was he. He claimed that his tongue could be the cure to her lack of sexual desire. "Oh baby, that is so sad. All you need is the right man. I promise my tongue would change your mind." It was like he believed that one lick would cause Lauren to pack her bags, kiss her Mum goodbye and pursue a career in Amsterdam in the red-light district. Someone needs to call the President. We need to send this man's tongue to the Middle East; he can lick it into peace.

Unfortunately, the Middle East remains as un-licked and war-torn as ever, as does Lauren, minus the war-torn aspect. It seemed that despite his most generous offers of oral sex and human board games Lauren decided that her heart lay elsewhere. Grant was not her Rich Uncle Moneybags which as a fantastic news as a relationship would have sounded a bit incestuous. Lauren and Grant parted ways; however, Lauren never saw her small, metal hat again.

One Man's Dream Is Every

Woman's Nightmare

I think one of the most obvious ways to tell an individual has become old is when even their dreams become dull as fuck. I had a manager that hated me. Well, to be perfectly honest, I have had many managers who have hated me for some unknown reason. Don't ask me why as I am rather obviously a fucking delight to work with. Nonetheless, there was this one manager who despised me. I mean he would consistently be a complete and utter wanker to me at every feasible opportunity. I once, having worked at the store for about a month and having no idea where anything was, asked him where a product was for a customer. In front of said customer he retorted "You are not the cleverest person, are you?" to which even the customer looked at me like 'what the fuck did that motherfucker just say about you?'

I think most people unfortunately encounter this kind of employer at some point in their work life. Well, it seems my personal knobhead clawed his way into my dreams. I did not butcher him in sheer rage, nor did we make sweet love in the canteen. He simply said "Hello," to me next to the water cooler and then I awoke. Lame as fuck, I know. That is how I know I have become old.

However, John at the age of 67-years-old did not have this bed time issue. He may have not slept dry for an entire night in several years but he had decent dreams. His dreams were full of excitement. He dreamt of slaying dragons, riding a shark butt naked into a volcano and eating ice cream with a bikini clad Dalek. Whilst these all do indeed sound rather riveting, the dream this tale is centred around is considerably more mundane in comparison. This dream, like so many before and after it, was about a woman. The woman was named Jasmine. She was 34, brunette, athletic, tall and a devoted mother of two. I realise that seems oddly specific for a dream; let me explain.

What made this dream about this beautiful woman more incredible is that John had never met Jasmine. Nonetheless, there she was in his dreams. At least that is what John told Jasmine when he found her on a dating app Jasmine was confused about the existence of John in her inbox. After all, she had set the boundaries for a match at a max age of 40. Now Jasmine was no math teacher, but she was rather adamant that 67 was in fact a little bit higher than 40. Although, if anyone has an alternative mathematical viewpoint to Jasmine and myself, please email   IDONTGIVEAFUCK@NOTONEBIT.FU.   His appearance could be explained by the fact that his age was in fact set on his profile to 37. It turns out John was not a math teacher either.

John continued in vain to woe the woman of his dreams: "On a good day Jasmin, I'd fall clumsily at your feet and say forgive me it is not my legs that have given way but my heart and I'd know from that point there would be no future, for I would be forever stuck in the moment I met you."

Wow, Jasmine said to herself, *this one is a real charmer. I'd better buy a dress for the wedding... or for his funeral. Whatever comes first.*

However, I, the author of this text, am curious about one element of this statement. Let's examine this section: he states that on a 'good day' it is not his 'legs' that have 'given way' but his 'heart'. So, when we condense what has been said it translates to 'on the best of days, I will have a fatal heart attack and admit my undying love for a total stranger'. With that understood, what the fuck occurs on a bad day? I theorise that it consists of John unsheathing his penis from his piss-stained trousers and yelling "charge!" as he runs into the crowded cheese aisle at Sainsbury's.

However, this romance, which let's be honest so far sounded full of hope and promise, was doomed. John noted that Jasmine was too far away; she lived about 80 miles from him. One must conclude that there was not a direct bus route to her location. Jasmine said dumbfounded "I would travel anywhere for true love."

To which John said, with an amount of confidence and bullish bravado that was not yet earned, "Yeah, but that is because you are young and daft? Do you love me, Jasmin?"

First, of all her name is J-A-S-M-I-N-E not J-A-S-M-I-N. Yes, the difference is one letter but that is the difference between her name and the local town's weirdo's name, who talks to the ducks naked with bread attached to her bare chest. It really is not hard to write her name correctly, is it? It is written at the top of the dating app, the app you are using to communicate with her. It is a mere glance upwards and even, for the self-confessed woman of your dreams, you cannot be fucked to even try. Also, 'daft' to most is not considered a positive adjective to describe someone. For instance, it would be incredibly 'daft' that a total stranger, who has just insulted a woman's intelligence, lied about his age and spelt her name wrong, would expect her to somehow love him. Now that... that would be daft. Very, very, daft indeed.

The Rich Bitch

Jessica was rich. Not a little bit rich, but a lot rich. Her father did stuff. I am unsure about what this 'stuff' entailed. Jessica tried to elaborate to me but, as it turns out, my feeble, little brain could not entirely comprehend the intricate complexities. So it will therefore remain labelled as 'stuff'. Nonetheless, the consensus is that he earned a rather extortionate amount of money.

Jessica's father's wealth meant that herself and her mother were well looked after. However, this does not mean Jessica was your stereotypical 'rich bitch' seen on [insert trashy reality show here]. Instead, she was intelligent, down to Earth, humorous and charitable. One of the benefits of her wealth was that her mother could take her on numerous excursions as a child, of which her most favourite was trips to the stately homes. The grandeur, majestic architecture and overall majesty of these homes engrossed and enthralled the young princess that laid dormant within Jessica.

Jessica's love of these stately homes only deepened with age and she would often visit them in her spare time as a young, successful business woman.   Therefore, when Jessica first went on a dating app she decided to include 'stately homes' in her bio as a hobby. After all, it seemed important to be upfront about this particular interest of hers and it would also be, at a bare minimum, an interesting talking point.

Turns out no one noticed this unusual interest of hers. Men seemed more interested in, to be blunt, her looks, chest and bum. It was almost like the men of the online world did not read her bio but assessed her on looks alone. No, I refuse to believe it. Men are not that shallow. Well... no, not all of them are... at least Enter Malcolm into the frame, who somehow made Jessica wish she'd found a mere shallow, sex obsessed knobhead.

"I see you like stately homes," Malcolm exclaimed with excitement "I've seen a fair few myself."

Oh, Jessica thought happily, *finally someone I can have an interesting and engaging conversation with that isn't about sex.*

Oh, Jessica. Poor, naive Jessica. Have you not read my sensational book called *Tales from The Online Dating Zoo*?

If you had, you would know that it always turns into sex with these fuckheads.

"I saw Buckingham Palace on that show *The Crown* and it was the most badly decorated stately home I have ever seen."

"Oh ok," Jessica said, deflated 'This man is an absolute imbecile'.

First of all, *The Crown* was obviously not filmed at Buckingham Palace. The Queen cannot be seen in a deleted blooper chowing down on a stuffed crust meat feast Domino's pizza whilst watching her favourite movie, *Saw: The Final Chapter*. It was instead shot inside a multitude of other stately homes and expensive studio sets. What is more, whilst Jessica had never seen the inside of Buckingham Palace, she could not imagine anyone thinking to themselves, *ohhhhhh, someone has raided Ikea's Bargain corner,* at the interior design of the Queen's abode.

Fuck it, let's see what more this wannabe historian has to offer, Jessica said to herself through gritted teeth.

"Yeah, it looks like a freshly shaved minge; a real hacked-up bush," Malcolm said with an evident air of intelligence and sophistication. This is quite possibly the oddest simile I have ever encountered, bearing in mind my job here is essentially to come up with the oddest similes imaginable. For those who are naïve or curious, I do not believe Malcolm meant the artistic bush shaping found in horticulture but instead, meant the trimming of pubic hair.

"Well..." Jessica started with a mixture of dumbfounded curiosity and anger at how the conversation had ventured from Buckingham Palace to the subject matter of pubic hair "Mine is rather sloppy and hacked up." She wanted to mention this fact in case her fictional lacklustre personal grooming would be a deal breaker. She continued "I am not the best at shaving. It is like handing the razor blade to Edward Scissorhands and hoping for the best."

"Yum!" which was not a reaction Jessica had even considered "Who can resist a bit of blood and some stray long pubes?"

"Welcome to Who Wants to Win a Hundred Euros and a Packet of Wine Gums with your host the one, the only The Divorced Dad."

"Hello everyone and welcome back. Last time we left on a real cliff hanger. Jason here was about to walk away with our grand prize of a whopping hundred euros and, more importantly, a packet of, now half eaten, Wine Gums. All he has to do is answer one question: who can resist a bit of blood and some stray long pubes?"

"Oh, I just don't know. I should know this; pubic hair is my topic of expertise. I just have no real clue. I am going to go on a real limb here. It is an absolute head scratcher but I am going to follow my gut. God, my Mum is going to kill me if I get this wrong, she had her heart set on eating those Wine Gums. The pressure is unreal when you are actually in the hot seat, isn't it? Huh, umm... my final answer: is: C, everyone, everyone can resist it."

The ever-adventurous Malcolm honed in on the mention of Johnny Depp's iconic scissor infused character and surmised that hand jobs must be a total nightmare for someone like Jessica with blades as hands. However, he became relieved when he came to the conclusion that their relationship could be exclusively blowjobs. Jessica simply wrote 'No' and, when probed for more details, she diligently catered to Malcolm's wishes explaining that she had rows of sharp piranha-like teeth that would make short work of his small, measly maggot.

Jasper the Unfriendly Ghost

I sit here about to write this tale at the onset of Autumn. The darkness of October has started to crawl in to consume what little warmth remains from the dregs of Summer. A bitter wind, doused with a blanket of unwelcome rain, batters the trees. Their leaves, once full of life, have now fallen onto the dank floor to form a brown mound of rot and decay. A noise that curls the toes of all who hear it echoes outside. Is it merely the weather or a demonic creature from our deepest, darkest fears?

All this dark and dim talk seems like a marvellous time to tell a terrifying, scary story. So, settle in, huddle together under a blanket, turn up the heating, prepare some comfort food and be set for a real scare.

The moon shone down onto a dark, deserted road. The citizens of the nearby towns knew the road that bordered them all too well. The legends, the rumours and now the recent first-hand accounts had damned that stretch of tarmac that laid between Tallas and Dorndon to be practically abandoned.

The drivers who did brave the road were so focused on finding the exit that none looked a direction but forward. The remains of the lone traveller were illuminated for all to see, but no one looked. No one had seen the slim blade glisten in the moonlight as the spectral assailant tore out the man's throat....

"Woah, woah, woah, I did not mean that kind of ghost story. For Christ's sake that is the last time I leave the laptop unattended; I have told you time and time again Stephanie Queen that this is not a horror book. I don't care if your dad is the maestro of horror, this is a book about weirdo's, perverts and their unfortunate antics. End of."

This tale is, in fact, about the act of ghosting in the online dating world. "What the fuck is that?", I hear you ask. Well, to most, it is the ultimate dating crime. A heinous, unforgivable act that should be punished with the utmost form of torture: a twelve-hour *Peppa Pig* marathon.

Picture this, if you will. You have had an endless stream of unsuccessful romances but you have, against all seeming probability, found someone that could be the one. Their words melt the cold caverns of the heart, their smile makes the world feel ablaze with wonder and their handsome looks flutter your fanny. You talk for hours... an end to the flow of conversation seems unimaginable. You tell them your most intimate desires, hopes and dreams. Could this be the real deal?

Harriet met Jasper on a popular online dating platform. They got on like a house on fire, minus all the death, livelihoods lost and irreversible destruction. That destruction was all still to come.

A date was set for these two love birds to meet for a drink and break that initial ice. Who knows, if all went well then a nice dinner and a sea front walk headed towards her bedroom could be on the cards. However, Harriet wanted to make sure. As evidenced in this book, all too often some deceitful individuals can catfish a match. The art of the filter is a well-known tool in the catfish's arsenal as is the use of other people's pictures entirely. One minute, a Zac Effron look alike is talking to you about his intense workout schedule only for the magic of filters to dissolve and reveal Slimer from *Ghostbusters*, munching through some trash.

To solve this cautious distrust, a video call was scheduled. The call went well, or so Harriet believed. If one had a checklist titled 'elements of a successful video call' then all elements would be checked. The conversation flowed as well as it did in text. He was handsome and articulate. What is more, he seemed nice.

Fast forward a fun filled few hours, Jasper said his farewells and told Harriet they would talk more tomorrow. Tomorrow came and Harriet text her beloved 'Thanks for a lovely chat last night, hope you are okay this morning?'. *Simplistic, caring and casual,* thought Harriet as she started her car for her commute to work. Lunchtime came and Harriet was about to take a bite out of her sandwich when she remembered to check her texts. Nothing. *Well,* she started to think of an excuse, *he must be hectic at work.* 3pm, nothing. 5pm, nothing. 7pm... oh wait... nothing. Then her worst fears were confirmed, her text had been read. That little blue tick stared deep into her soul and and muttered with malice "he's active now."

Harriet sent a brief reminder to Jasper that she hadn't yet received a response. Still, she received no word. And with that she came to the conclusion that Jasper, the apparent, friendliest ghost was a complete bell end. Yes, he had ghosted her. The conversations, the promises, the secrets, the 'nice guy' persona and the sexual tension all were lies.

The real cause of hurt comes from the lack of closure. Of course, he was entitled not to like her. He had free will after all, however, the lack of reason is sheer cowardice. A million worries crossed Harriet's mind: did he not like her hilarious childhood anecdotes? Was the conversation about her dad too much? Did he think she was too well spoken? Was she ugly? The truth is, Harriet would never find out these answers and that is where the true hurt lies. Rather than wallow she decided to exorcise Jasper from her life, delete his number and remove him from social media.

It has been fourteen months since he said his last, and final, words to Harriet. He still haunts her heart, but nonetheless she has moved on. She has found her one. He will not leave all of a sudden or vanish like Houdini. He is here, and she doesn't need a Sixth Sense to know that.

The End of the Tour

The wheels come to a sudden halt as the mud-covered tour vehicle stuttered and stalled into the station.

Here we are folks, the end. It has been one hell of an adventure. I am not ashamed to admit I am a little bit teary. We have delved head first into The Online Dating Zoo and survived all the horrors, wonders and anomalies of human nature that inhabit its enclosures.

Ron Gammon stumbled out the car door with a loud thud. Since the commencement of this wretched tour, Mr.

Gammon had downed several bottles of an unknown, discount alcohol labelled 'The Stuff'. It turns out expense was most definitely spared on this tour-de-shite. He was, for lack of better words, shit faced drunk.

 "The... uh, The... umm, Diabetic Dad? No, no, no... you are that divorced loser, fuck, The Divorced Dad. Yeah, that's it. I knew that, I knew that. What do you think... about... uh, all this? Fucking brilliant, isn't it?" he belched, his breath stinking of an unholy cocktail of scotch egg and vomit.

However, this drunk imbecile does raise a rather interesting question: what do I think about all of this? In the words of Yoda, "Conclude we must."

***

Alas, I hear those countless voices. The chorus of chants that demand "One more tale," as if I was some kind of

Rock'n'roll God. These cries for more deafen me, but no dearest of readers, it is time. It is time to end this tour into the bowels of Hell, for I can write no more about the trials and tribulations of dating apps.

First of all, can we have one massive, heartfelt round of applause to the anonymous submitters that have filled this book with their hilarious, horrific and unfortunately, all too relatable anecdotes. I would like to express my heartfelt gratitude to you all as, in all honesty, this book would have been utter shit without your contributions. I truly wish that the horrendous experiences you endured are a mere blip in a lifetime of unimaginable happiness. To anyone who has submitted a tale that did not feature in this book please know the task of selection was unbelievably difficult. However, I have laughed and cried at almost every entry sent to me, but some seemed easier to write than others for a multitude of reasons. With that said, who knows what the future entails? Could these stories possibly be the foundation of a follow up expedition into the wilderness of online dating?

I think a heartfelt thanks wrapped in the grandest of beautiful bows needs to also be delivered to each and every member of The Divorced Dad Facebook page. Thank you, Tony. Thank you, Harriet. Thank you, Terry. Thank you, Pauline. Thank you, Gwen. Bear with me a second there are about 12,000 individuals to thank, this could take some time. Thank you, Scott. Thank you, Sharon. Thank you, Shirley. Thank you, Adam.

I do not want to sound overdramatic but every single one of you unknowingly played a part in saving a life. Not only would this book or The Divorced Dad page not exist but there is a real chance I would not be here right now without you. I was at the lowest point of my life, fresh from a divorce and a total mental breakdown, when I started to write my ramblings like a madman to absolutely no one. Then no one became someone, the followers started to trickle and then flood in. All of a sudden, I felt I had a new sense of worth. I became a porpoise with a purpose. The purpose: to make a bunch of weirdos (no offence) like myself laugh even in the shittiest of times. You all unwittingly became my therapy and now I am thrilled to announce that, for the first time, in a long time, I feel better. So, thank you, from the bottom of my heart I mean that.

Next, let's address the blue whale dressed in a tutu that is beached in the corner of the room. I am sure that one of the central criticisms of this book will be that it seems rather anti-men. First of all, this was not the intention. No, the aim of this book was to deliver a fair and unbiased examination of online dating. I admit, on that front, I have failed. I will be the first to concede this collection of stories has not coloured the males of the online world in the best shade. In fact, if one was to look at a Dulux paint colour chart, the shade that would be most similar is labelled 'Shit Creek', a repugnant brown, which is a colour scheme that no one would want in their bathroom or kitchen.

However, I remain adamant that I indeed tried. I asked on countless occasions for submissions from men. In return I received a total of four, two of which were from friends. Meanwhile, there was a biblical flood of women who told me of their woes, frustrations and horrors.

Therefore, one can assume three plausible hypotheses from this information:

1. The audience of The Divorced Dad are predominantly female.

2. Men are not as willing to share their experiences

3. Women do indeed experience the vast majority of abuse from online dating

Let's tackle these in chronological order, number one is most likely correct. Whilst I do not have the data to ascertain the complete gender makeup of the audience of The Divorced Dad, because, let's be honest, who can be fucked to know? I can make an educated guess based on the mass number of females that like and comment on posts. Yes, sometimes I really do feel like the only sausage in the factory.

As for the second point, as discussed before in 'Baggage Claims', men do not like to share their emotions or issues. Therefore, there is a real possibility that a mass number of men do have stories about women who have mistreated, harassed and over-sexualised them, but are too ashamed to come forward. There very well may be men who have had women state they want to ride their shaft like a fleshy pogo stick. Alas, I am yet to encounter such a claim.

The final theory is the most complicated to discuss. Yes, I do indeed believe women experience the brunt of abuse on online dating platforms. I feel that is undeniable. But why? I refuse to state that males, as a whole, are the issue. I know that is controversial but hear me out. Indeed, some men are the issue, such men as seen in these tales. However, there are incredible men out there who genuinely want to find love and romance. When I was on a dating app as a 'woman' there was at least three nice, well-intentioned men for every heinous, horrendous prick. However, it is unfortunate that stories about nice men seem to lack a comedic wow factor, otherwise, this book would be with littered with them. Therefore, it is my humble opinion that the real issue is assholes and these individuals are not male exclusive. After all, we all know a few female assholes.

I will, however, state that there are more male assholes in the world then female. One only needs to look towards the news to realise that. The reason for this, at a guess, is history. There are traits we view as a modern, educated culture as obscene, horrific and offensive that were valued mere centuries ago in men. For instance, aggression was seen as a benefit for annihilating rival tribes and striking fear into those who dare defy them.

Now, if Callum calls someone the irredeemable C-word and threatened to 'kick the shit' out of someone, he would be viewed as a bell end. This physically aggressive streak has no real benefit in a civilised and relatively safe world and therefore, has been subdued in most. With that said we learn from our elders and if none before us have taken the initiative to halt these unneeded, offensive traits then unfortunately they usually remain in the current generation like an incurable virus. Thus, an asshole is born, unfortunately Lady Gaga declined my offer to star in this side movie project.

Now with that said, these asshole traits for most are dormant, however, online dating starts an unusual internal reaction in some. The root cause of this is: anonymity. One of the best, and also worst, features of online dating is we get to socialise with total strangers.

However, this does remove the personal aspect out of the human experience. The individuals we talk to become nothing more than strings of data which, unless we choose to, we never have to meet. This for some individuals means that there are no consequences to their actions and thus allows them to treat others in the most horrendous means.

So, what do I think of the current state of online dating? To be honest, it scares me. I have tried to write a 'hilarious' book, to limited success, to make readers smile after some of the worst times in modern history. However, the truth is these stories are horrific. Each one of these tales is an example of the abuse, harassment and dehumanisation of a real, living breathing human being with feelings and emotions. It outrages and hurts me that individuals are treated to this kind of debasement in the search for love.

Now, I do believe the original intention of the first online dating platforms were honest and decent: a safe haven to find and connect with a soul mate. However, it is safe to say that this is no longer the case. The owners of these platforms are not naïve either and know all of this, however, it is allowed to continue almost unchallenged. It seems hypocritical to me that if an individual approached someone on the streets and said a grotesque, sexual remark then the authorities would most likely become involved. In stark contrast, in the online world the worst that is to be expected is a temporary account suspension and a potential slap on the wrist.

As a side note, to those individuals sat there who think that this is not an issue. The ones who simply shrug and say "so what?". Then listen up fuck nuts: one day your daughter or granddaughter, or even great granddaughter, will start to date online and there will be these assholes who will harass and sexualise them. Is that the future we want for our kids? If so, I would like to offer you a heartfelt fuck you, you absolute total cum stain of insignificance.

***

The tour group stood in the still to be built visitor centre. Ron looked at me bewildered. To be honest, this feat did not seem difficult. He seemed like the kind of man who would be baffled if someone stole his nose. However, to Mr. Gammon's credit I had acted rather weird for the last ten minutes as I had been stood motionless in silence as I concluded this entire experience inside my head (wink, wink).

Ron started "uh, so..."

At that moment, a loud smash echoed around the desolate, husk of a visitor centre. A bloodcurdling scream could be heard from somewhere in the distance. An alarm blared. The exhibits were loose.

A moment later three male exhibits had surrounded us. We were cornered and defenceless. One user snorted "Cor, look what we have here lads," as he removed a small metal cat from his ass.

"Oh, it looks like a fine piece of arse here, Rodney," another murmurs as he clutches a pair of Sainsbury's own brand lingerie to his nose.

"Ripe for the taking I would say," was shouted from above us from the mouth of a man attached to the roof via an anal hook. This was the inevitable end of The Online Dating Zoo. This could be the end of The Divorced Dad.

Then all of a sudden, another crash. This time it was a welcomed sound. The anal hook had detached and the rubble, and once said hooked man, slammed down onto the men down below, it seems someone must not have read their anal hook rule book.

I survived. The Divorced Dad lives. The Online Dating Zoo, however, laid in ruins as we were evacuated out of the failed attraction. A 20ft man with ostrich feathers stuck out of his bum roared as the helicopter started its ascent home. Ron looked at me and tried to continue our conversation from earlier "so, uh what, what do, uh, you think?"

I looked outside at the destruction and the now free to roam exhibits who were headed towards the nearest town to harass more women "Well Mr. Gammon, after careful consideration, I've decided not to endorse your zoo."

References

1. 'How to Use an Anal Hook' (no date) Uberkinky, Available at: https://www.uberkinky.com/essential-guides/how-to-use-ananal-hook.html (Accessed 27/03/21) 283

2. Ibid

3. Ibid

4. Ibid

5. 'The 4 Rules of Bird Watching' (No date) Listen2Articles, Available at: https://www.listen2articles.com/hobbies/birdwatching/the-4-rules-of-bird-watching/ (Accessed 17/06/21)

6. Leelo, Jamie, 2016, 'The Definitive List of Christmas-Themed Dirty Talk Phrases', Elite Daily, Available at: https://www.elitedaily.com/dating/sex/dirty-talk/1732930 (Accessed 13/08/21)

7. Ibid

8. Ibid

9.   Ibid

10.   Ibid

11.   Ibid

12. 1. Define The Relationship 2. See You For Sex 3. Want To Trade Pictures 4. Down To Fuck 5. Talk Dirty To Me 6. Are You Horny? 7. Cum In Mouth 8. Ass To Mouth 9. Get Nude On Cam 10. Drug And Disease Free

13.   Soh, Debra, '1 in 6 People Has a Sex Fetish- Here Are A Few of the Craziest' Available at: https://www.womenshealthmag.com/sex- andlove/a19976035/extreme-fetishes-0/ (Accessed 12/10/21)

14.   Ibid

THE END

Acknowledgements

Well holy shit, I have somehow finished writing this book. It was fucking hard. Actually, scratch that it was incredibly fucking hard. Luckily, I had the most incredible bunch of human beings as support. This is indeed the page of soppy shit...

First of all, I need to thank my sprogs. No, to be honest they offered little aid in the creation of this book, however, they constantly provide me with an endless barrage of smiles, love and laughter. In the same breath I feel I also to thank the ex, that old shrew (I am just kidding). She is without doubt the best ex-wife a man could ever ask for and continues to be one of my best friends.

On the topic of friends, I have the greatest in the world. From Pete to Frankie these wonderful individuals feel me to the brim with an insane amount of warmth and love. I also need to thank my family who tolerated me at my worst and still tolerate me at my best.

To all those who submitted their stories. Thank you so, so very much, without them this book would be rather bare bones. It is an absolute honour to be able to tell your stories and I hope I have done them justice.

A massive heartfelt thanks to Meryl Whittington who proof read this very book in your hands. Without her sheer determination this would be a dire mess of grammatical errors and spelling mistakes.

I cannot forget to thank my incredible other half who has supported me throughout and provided me with endless encouragement. What is more she makes me smile, laugh and enjoy life. What more can you humanly ask for?

The final person to thank is my partner in crime: Sam Felstead. She aided me in my initial journey into the dark realms of online dating and helped me to respond the initial batch of internet weirdos.

Printed in Great Britain
by Amazon